DAN CLARKE

Bitcoin

The Complete Guide to the World's Most Popular Cryptocurrency

First edition

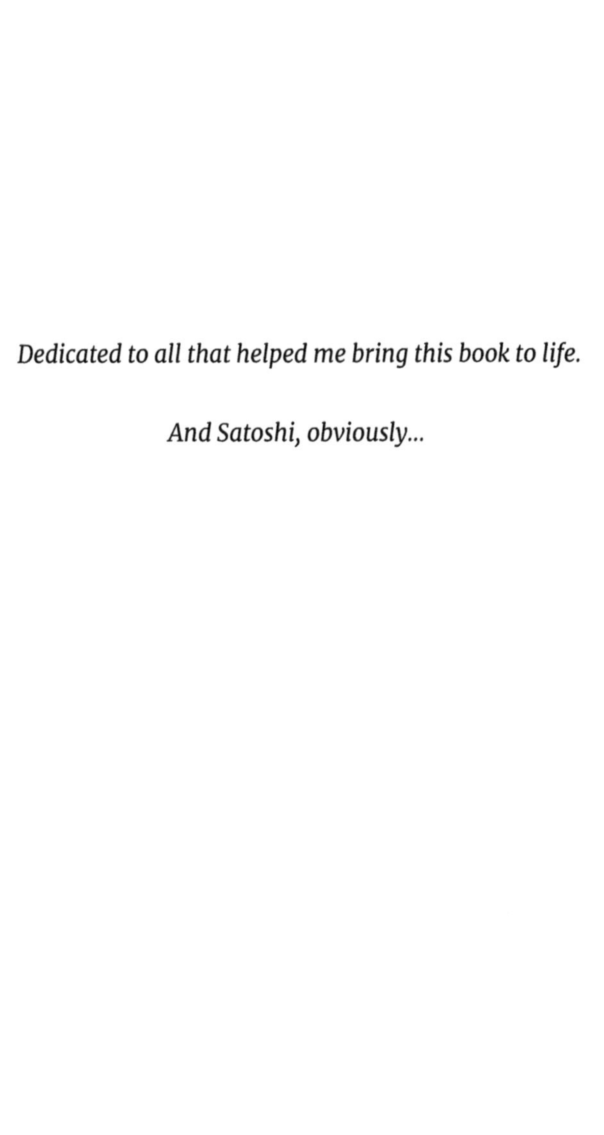

Dedicated to all that helped me bring this book to life.

And Satoshi, obviously...

Contents

Foreword

I grew up in a working-class family in a former coal mining town in northern England, far removed from high finance. At 17, I left school and took on various jobs—from packing boxes in a warehouse and working at McDonald's to serving as a police officer.

At 20, battling a tough depression, I made a bold decision: sell all my belongings, grab a backpack, and fly to Berlin with nothing but a one-way ticket and a backpack. Landing in Berlin during the summer of 2008, amidst a global economic collapse, was both daunting and refreshing. I didn't know anyone and couldn't speak German, but necessity and youthful overconfidence taught me a crucial life lesson early on:

'You're on your own, kid.'

Berlin in 2008 was as good a place as any to see through a once in a generation economic collapse. Beers were cheap, summers were long, and camaraderie among friends was strong despite our shared financial struggles. I dipped into the classic expat roles—teaching English and guiding pub crawls—before landing a job at a German tech company launching a product in the UK market. Despite not speaking German at the time, I excelled in Search Engine Optimisation (SEO), absorbing knowledge like a sponge while pursuing side projects like repairing and reselling Xboxes and flipping products on Amazon.

However, my pattern of leaving and being fired from jobs continued. I was headhunted by Groupon, where I led global SEO operations during its meteoric rise to a $36 billion company listed on the New York Stock Exchange.

Eager for new challenges, I moved to Dubai, worked with major marketing agencies, co-founded my own agency, and was fired again after two months.

In 2015 I again packed up and flew to Kuala Lumpur, then Singapore, where I started another agency. Lacking a university degree, I decided to join Mensa which secured me an employment visa, enabling me to collaborate with global tech firms and the Singaporean government for three years.

In 2017, I discovered Bitcoin—a turning point that merged my technical skills, entrepreneurial spirit, and passion for financial innovation. I traded my life savings for bitcoin and other cryptocurrencies, getting involved working on marketing and growth projects.

Through a friend of mine I was referred to a job at Binance in 2018. I interviewed but they told me they had filled the position.

I couldn't take 'no' for an answer so I sat down and wrote a 30 page audit of the Binance website with everything they could fix, and how.

I got hired, and days later I was on a one way flight to Tokyo to start work.
Working at Binance was exhilarating as the company grew into a multi-billion-dollar crypto industry pillar. I hopped around Tokyo, Shanghai, Singapore, Jakarta, and Bali for two years.

I moved on to a project with friends, only to be fired and embroiled in lawsuits.

My next roles at Gemini with the Winklevoss twins, Polygon, and BitGet followed a similar pattern of rapid growth and unexpected layoffs.

Reflecting on the past fifteen years, my journey has been nothing short of incredible. From getting blackout drunk with North Korean spies in Pyongyang to navigating the Taliban-occupied Tribal Area region of Pakistan in a bomb-proof van with armed guards, and riding a motorbike solo across Indonesia, my experiences have been diverse and surreal.

Through Bitcoin, I've earned millions and lost them too, including a $2 million loss in half an hour—a moment that remains one of the most surreal experiences of my life.

Writing this book took two years, outlasting two relationships and five different apartments. It has been a profound learning experience, more so than anything else I've done in the industry. Today, I travel around Asia, motorcycling, scuba diving, investing, and enjoying downtime with friends.

I extend my gratitude to all who have supported me on this

journey. Special thanks to my friends across Asia—Myles, Rhod, Steve, Marius, Matt, Dave, Jarrad, Chris, and Jon—for their unwavering support.

1

What is Money?

> *"That money talks, I'll not deny, I heard it once: It said, 'Goodbye'."*
> – Richard Armour

Before understanding Bitcoin, we need to take a step back and ask a bigger question.

What is money? On its surface, this sounds like a stupid question, right?
Everyone knows what money is. It's the folded picture of the Queen poking out from your wallet, or the bundled stack of dead presidents sitting on your table.
It's the numbers beaming back to you from your online banking app, or the bottom right corner of your payslip.

Society is split across a spectrum between those that 'have' money and those that don't. Money motivates people where other methods can't. It's said that 'money makes the world go round'. But what *is* money?

At its heart, money is nothing more than a collectively agreed-upon delusion—a delusion that society accepts to form the cornerstone of productive commerce and the governance of civilisation as a whole.

Today the most commonly understood form of money is probably the United States Dollar. These come in various denominations, from $1 up to $100 notes (also referred to as bills). A single $100 note is simply a thin slip of paper and fabric with markings on it—a picture of Benjamin Franklin, the number 100, the inscription 'THIS NOTE IS LEGAL TENDER FOR ALL DEBTS, PUBLIC AND PRIVATE,' and the signatures of two government officials.

Inherently, it has almost no value. You can't realistically eat it, you can't realistically wear it, and if you burned it, you'd get a trivial amount of heat. Its value stems entirely from its value in exchange for other real world goods or services.

You can take that $100 note and exchange it for 5-6 hours of manual labour from a worker, or a tailored suit, or a bicycle. These are items that all have clear inherent value. So why would anyone accept an inert slip of paper and fabric in return for their valuable time or goods?

That is because of the collective idea that we all hold in society that the USD is one of the best items to use as a medium of exchange and a store of value. The lady who sells you a bicycle for your $100 note doesn't actually want the note itself; she wants the purchasing power it represents. She can later exchange it for a new coat for her son, food for a week, or whatever else she desires. That is the power of the USD as a medium of exchange.

Consider this: Open your wallet and take out the first banknote you find.

Ask yourself, 'Is this banknote ever really mine? Or is it just my turn to spend it?'

Imagine, then, a world in which USD and other currencies didn't exist. I'm sure you either have a job currently or have previously, in which you expend your labour to produce goods or services; to make this example easier, let's assume you are a baker who bakes bread. Each day you work and produce 100 loaves of bread, and you need fuel to power your baking ovens. You go across town to the fuel store and want to pick up a bag of coal to fuel your ovens, but without an agreed instrument of exchange you're left negotiating with the fuel store to accept x loaves of bread in return for a sack of coal.

How many loaves of bread is a sack of coal worth? Who knows, there's no real market for that kind of trade. Worse still, what if a rival baker has already been to the store and exchanged ten loaves of bread for a sack of coal? The fuel salesmen will sadly tell you 'I have more bread than I could possibly need! I won't accept any bread as payment!'

The whole system of commerce falls apart very quickly, and

that is with something as tangible as loaves of bread, I imagine attempting to exchange hours of website optimisation consultancy with store selling coal would be a much shorter and less productive conversation.

This is what economists call the 'double coincidence of wants' problem; in order for a trade to take place, you need a double coincidence of wants—that is, the baker wants coal and the coal seller wants bread. When there is no double coincidence of wants, then there is no trade and society as a whole is unable to make productive progress.

Money in the form of banknotes and coins solves this problem by removing one side of the double coincidence of wants problem. This is possible because the coins or notes serve as both a medium of exchange—i.e., they can be exchanged for goods and services—and a store of value.
The coal seller does not want your bread but will accept your $100 note because he knows he can store value in the note and later exchange it for goods or services he desires.

The $100 note has no inherent value, but is widely accepted as a medium of exchange by a substantial number of parties and will retain its value over time until he needs to exchange it for something else.

For this system to work, all that is required is that society as a whole believes in the store of value and medium of exchange. This requires that the money supply cannot be debased by the issuance of more $100 notes, either through forgery or mismanagement of the issuing authority.

Commodities as Money

Paper money is a relatively new invention in the history of the world. Historically people have used other materials to solve the 'double coincidence of wants' problem.

Gold has historically been used as both a store of value and a medium of exchange, and there are many good reasons that make gold very suitable for this purpose.

Firstly, gold is robust and versatile; it does not perish or tarnish over time and is resistant to the elements. Secondly, the rate at which new gold is mined has remained remarkably stable over time at around 2% of the total supply, which prevents the circulating supply from being meaningfully debased. The rate of inflation of supply is both known and stable.

These features make gold a good store of value over a long period of time. In fact, it is said that one ounce of gold could purchase a tailored suit 250 years ago, and an ounce of gold would still be sufficient to purchase a tailored suit today.

Other commodities have been used as money too. Famously, in ancient Rome, soldiers were often paid in salt—a scarce and useful commodity in the ancient world—which is believed to be where the modern word 'salary' is derived from. Their monthly allowance was called 'salarium' ('sal' being the Latin word for salt).

More commonly, gold was used as the primary medium of exchange and store of value. In ancient Rome they minted coins from gold called aurei.

Each of which held a value of 25 silver coins called denarii.

Whilst these coins would have been considered high technology in their time, they would be trivially easy to replicate today, and their low-quality production opened them to issues of counterfeiting and debasement.
One of the more common forms of debasement of coins in this time was through a process known as 'coin clipping'. Coin clipping is the process whereby a person would clip a small chunk of the base metal of the coin away from the body of the coin itself. If you take 100 coins and clip 1% off each coin, the impact on each individual coin would be barely noticeable. However, the total of the removed metal could be melted down and formed into a new coin, turning your 100 coins into 101 and debasing the monetary supply by a small percentage.

To counteract this, Isaac Newton, when appointed Master of the Mint of Great Britain in 1699, introduced the idea of adding an inscription and design on the edges of coins to prevent the practice of chipping away the edge.

This remains in practice today and, despite no longer being minted from gold, is the origin of why UK Pound coins still have the phrase *DECUS ET TUTAMEN* engraved on their edges. The phrase is Latin for 'ornament and a safeguard' - a safeguard against their debasement through clipping.

The Gold Standard

Given the inherent problems with the use of coins minted directly from precious metals, over time a better solution to these problems was sought. Whilst paper money had existed in the Far East from as early as the 7th century, only to be abolished later due to inflation, it was not until the 17th century that paper money would come into circulation in the Western world.

At its core, the concept of paper money in the Western world is based on a simple idea. Using a system of trusted goldsmiths a person could deposit their gold to the goldsmith to keep custody of, and in return receive a signed receipt stating the amount of gold they had deposited. The real innovation came in making these receipts redeemable by anyone who held the receipt—thus creating the first-ever instance of a 'bearer bond.'

Bearer bonds are, today, common financial instruments in the modern world and rely on the principle that whoever is holding the bond is able to redeem the underlying asset.

In 17th Century England, I might deposit £10 of gold to a goldsmith and receive 10 x £1 deposit receipts promising to pay the bearer of the receipt £1 in gold. With this I could then go to merchants in the town and exchange my bearer receipt for goods or services, and they would then either spend those receipts in the same way or choose to redeem them for the underlying gold directly from the goldsmith.

Over time banks were established to take the role of the counter-party to custody gold and issue banknotes. This led to the formal establishment of the world's oldest central bank, in Sweden, the 'Sveriges Riksbank' in 1668, followed rapidly by several banks in the United Kingdom—C. Hoare & Co. (1672), Barclays (1690), Coutts & Co. (1692)—and eventually the Bank of England in 1694.

For a time it was both perfectly legal, and commonplace, for multiple banks to issue their own bank notes that would be legal tender. Notably in the early days of the United States this practice gave birth to what has since been referred to as the 'Wildcat Banks' which were banks operating under state charters before there existed a nationalised banking system in the US. These banks would operate on state level charters and issue notes against your deposits. The problem of course became that any notes issued by these banks were always reliant upon the solvency of the bank and if that bank went bankrupt - as happened often - then your notes (which were simply claims against the banks deposits) would be worthless.

This is an important point to note. When depositing assets with any centralised party, your claim on those deposits is only as valid as the solvency of that institution. As we have seen in 2023 with the collapse of regional banks, this is a risk that remains as at the first signs of trouble, people flocked to move their funds out from the likes of Silicon Valley Bank, First Republic Bank, Signature bank, etc. despite them not even issuing their own bank notes.

This is not an issue isolated to the US; in fact, in the UK there remain several banks other than the Bank of England that are still able to issue banknotes, including some non-government entities:

Scotland:
- The Royal Bank of Scotland plc
- Bank of Scotland plc
- Clydesdale Bank plc

Northern Ireland:
- Bank of Ireland UK plc
- Danske Bank
- Ulster Bank Ltd
- Northern Bank Limited trading as Danske Bank

This practice is more commonly seen in Hong Kong, as anyone that has spent time in the territory would know. In Hong Kong all bank notes are issued by 3 non-government entities:

HSBC
Standard Chartered
Bank of China

Whilst all of these notes are redeemable at face value and are equally interchangeable, in a state that is referred to as 'fungible', they nonetheless all look noticeably different in appearance and design and are issued by entirely separate entities.

This is a hark back to the idea of banks issuing their own 'receipts' for their deposits held at the bank.

In most countries today the government maintains a monopoly on the issue of currency via some government connected monetary authority, such as the Monetary Authority of Singapore in

Singapore, or the Federal Reserve in the US. Though as we saw with the 2023 regional bank crisis, this issue transcends banks that issue banknotes and even causes fear in any institutions that hold funds above the government declared insured amounts.

Despite the fact that UK bank notes have not been redeemable for their underlying gold, to this day UK bank notes of all denominations have printed on them 'I PROMISE TO PAY THE BEARER ON DEMAND THE SUM OF' followed by the notes denomination.

Despite the fact that any of these notes are no longer redeemable for their face value of gold bullion.

The gold standard remained the cornerstone of western economies through until the mid 20th Century, when, one by one, governments across the western world suspended and then ultimately broke entirely with the redeemability of their bank notes for gold - ending once and for all the idea that circulating money was fully backed by gold reserves.

Perhaps one of the most famous instances of this came in 1933, in the United States when President Roosevelt issued the now infamous Executive Order 6102. Through the course of the great depression in the US the government came under strain, unable to issue more currency to ease the economic problems the country was facing. Given that the US Dollar was pegged to gold, the Federal Reserve was unable to issue more currency without taking custody of more gold with which to back it, without devaluing the rate at which the currency was redeemable for gold. Foreseeing this pending devaluation people in the US began to hold more gold in order to not have their savings devalued when the dollar would be reduced in value against gold, which the government of the day claimed was stalling the economy and worsening the effects of the global depression. On the 5th April 1933 President Roosevelt signed into effect Executive Order 6102 which, at the stroke of a pen, made private ownership of gold illegal in the United States and compelled anyone holding gold to hand it over to the government at a pre-determined and fixed rate of exchange for US Dollars of $20.67 per ounce.

Less than a year later the US Government passed the Gold Reserve Act 1934, devaluing the US Dollar to a rate of $35 USD per ounce, devaluing the US Dollar by over 40% against the underlying gold backing.

Through the course of the 20th Century western economies broke with their pegs to the gold standard. Sometimes temporarily at first, but ultimately permanently. The United Kingdom suspended the redeemability of bank notes for Gold in 1914 due to the financial strains on the economy from the first world war, before restoring the redeemability in 1925. This was seen as an issue of national pride by the then Chancellor of the Exchequer, Winston Churchill. This return to the gold standard was however short lived and the deflationary pressure it put on the currency ultimately led to it being abandoned again in 1931. From 1931 until 1944 the United Kingdom operated on an entirely 'fiat' system by which the currency in circulation was not backed by anything.

In 1944, towards the end of the second world war, the western world came together to reorganise their collective banking systems resulting in the Bretton Woods Agreement in which several countries agreed to back their national currencies with the US Dollar, which in turn was backed by gold at a rate of $35 per ounce, thus firmly establishing the US Dollar as the primary global reserve currency.

What happened in 1971?

The Bretton Woods Agreement held in place for over 25 years as western currencies pegged their value to the US Dollar which in turn was redeemable at the rate of $35 USD per ounce of gold. However, as we have seen throughout the ark of human history, a long and drawn out war once again put significant strain on government finances and put this gold peg at risk once again.

By the early 1970s the war in Vietnam had been running for some 15 years and the United States were increasingly locked in what appeared to be an expensive and unwinnable war. As we saw in WWII when the United Kingdom broke with the gold peg of the British pound, the United States too found itself in a position where it was forced to expand its monetary base to fund its war efforts. In 1971 the circulating supply of US dollars increased by 10% without any meaningful increase in the underlying gold bullion to back it. This had the de facto effect of devaluing the dollar against its gold reserves, however the Bretton Woods agreement held that all US Dollars were redeemable at a rate of $35 per ounce of gold. The agreement also held that the currencies of several western nations were pegged to the US Dollar and therefore also redeemable at the same rate for the underlying gold bullion.

The first cracks in this system came in May 1971 when the government of West Germany exited the Bretton Woods agreement and allowed its currency to freely float against the US Dollar. In the three months following its departure the West German Deutsche Mark rose 7.5% against the dollar as investors began to see that the US Dollar was no longer sufficiently backed by gold due to the increased issuance of dollars to fund the Vietnam war efforts.

As is common in any bank run, once panic sets in it is quickly followed by a stampede to take money out of the bank. In this case the bank was the US government and the money was the underlying gold reserves.

In July of 1971 the Swiss government redeemed $50m ($360m in 2023 dollars) of its US Dollar reserves for the underlying gold, The French government redeemed $191m ($1.38b in 2023 dollars). The floodgates were open and a full blown run on the US gold reserves.

In the face of this, the US Government took stark and unilateral action. On 15th August 1971 President Nixon took to the national airwaves and announced to the world that, with immediate effect, the United States would no longer redeem US Dollars for their underlying gold bullion.

> *The third indispensable element in building the new prosperity is closely related to creating new jobs and halting inflation. We must protect the position of the American dollar as a pillar of monetary stability around the world. In the past 7 years, there has been an average*

> *of one international monetary crisis every year... I have directed Secretary Connally to suspend temporarily the convertibility of the dollar into gold or other reserve assets, except in amounts and conditions determined to be in the interest of monetary stability and in the best interests of the United States. Now, what is this action—which is very technical—what does it mean for you? Let me lay to rest the bugaboo of what is called devaluation. If you want to buy a foreign car or take a trip abroad, market conditions may cause your dollar to buy slightly less. But if you are among the overwhelming majority of Americans who buy American-made products in America, your dollar will be worth just as much tomorrow as it is today. The effect of this action, in other words, will be to stabilize the dollar.*

– Richard Nixon, 15th August 1971

With this one move, the gold standard was broken for the final time in the western world and never again would the currency of any western country be backed by underlying gold reserves. The world was moved into the era of 'fiat' currencies.

From this day onwards, the US Dollar and other western currencies no longer adhered to the gold standard and became free floating currencies that essentially have no intrinsic value tied to anything. The currencies then hold value only based upon the faith and belief in the issuing authority or government that backs them. In practice this is enforced through both military might and the ability to enforce taxation on the productive labour of its population.

In the most obvious example, the United States Dollar is able to derive value from the requirement of a large number of people to be required to obtain it to pay their tax obligations to the government; but also the global system of trade, most notably the oil trade, being conducted in US Dollars requires people the world over to acquire US Dollars, which creates a strong demand for the currency.

Once again, at the heart of modern money we are back at where we began this chapter.
Money, it seems, is nothing more than a collective delusion we all buy into that numbers or pictures of the sovereign on slips of plastic in your pocket hold value. This collective delusion holds up modern society and facilitates global commerce so long as society continues to collectively agree that they hold value. Provided that the issuance and management of the currency is competently managed, this is a collective delusion that is fairly easily maintained, but there are countless examples of where mismanagement of the currency punctures this collective delusion and results in a rapid loss of confidence in the currency.

This was seen in the Weimar Republic in the 1920s, where the government printed money profligately and triggered hyper-inflation that collapsed the economy, or more recently in Zimbabwe, where the same fate met the Zimbabwean people as the government printed currency leading to runaway debasement and the ludicrous issuance of $100 trillion notes. A similar situation has been seen in the Venezuelan Bolívar, where the purchasing power of the currency has collapsed and it requires a suitcase full of banknotes to now buy a loaf of bread.

The modern world of fiat currencies is always in a fine balance, requiring careful management by the relevant authorities to avoid debasing them in ways that could lead to a loss of faith among the population that uses them. Unfortunately through the course of human history, almost every fiat currency has eventually ended in total collapse.

2

Origins of Bitcoin

> "Nothing is more powerful than an idea whose time has come."
>
> — Victor Hugo

Bitcoin's story begins in late 2008 with the publication of the Bitcoin whitepaper on 31st October—a 9-page, approximately 3,500-word document that lays out the fundamental workings of the Bitcoin network and bitcoins themselves. It is important to note the subtle distinction when describing Bitcoin. 'Bitcoin' with a capital 'B' refers to the network itself, whilst 'bitcoin' with a lowercase 'b' is used to describe the coins themselves.

In the whitepaper, Satoshi Nakamoto elegantly outlined in nine pages the entire concept and functionality of Bitcoin, covering the broad strokes of everything that manages the network today—from nodes to mining, issuance schedule, difficulty adjustment, and more.

Whilst some changes and upgrades to the code have been made over time, the distributed and permissionless nature of the system, and its mutually adversarial nature, makes any changes hard and long-drawn-out affairs, as we will cover later. As Satoshi himself pointed out in 2010 on the Bitcoin Talk forums

> *"The nature of Bitcoin is such that once version 0.1 was released, the core design was set in stone for the rest of its lifetime."*
>
> *– Satoshi Nakamoto*

It is hard to imagine there are many other documents of such short and concise form that have had a bigger impact on both the economic and political fabric of the world. By 2021, the entire cryptocurrency market cap reached a peak of almost $3 trillion. Within Amazon, it's reported that they don't consider new business ideas unless they can become at least a billion-dollar business. At $3 trillion, the Bitcoin whitepaper launched an entirely new industry in which every word of the document individually was worth almost a billion dollars.

Like many forces for good in the world, Bitcoin, in and of itself, was not an entirely new concept but rather drew together many existing ideas and technologies, corralling them into a system that was greater than the sum of its parts.

Similar to how the English language has been described by some for its co-opting and adoption of loanwords and influences from other languages, the development of Bitcoin can be considered to function similarly. While recent developments like BRC-20 tokens and Ordinals demonstrate Bitcoin's ongoing evolution and incorporation of external ideas, the original concept of Bitcoin also relied heavily on existing technologies.

It would certainly be fair, when describing Bitcoin's origins, to borrow a quote from our friend from the previous chapter:

> *"If I have seen further it is by standing on the shoulders of giants."*
> *– Sir Isaac Newton*

What makes Bitcoin revolutionary is both the way in which these technologies were incorporated together, and the political situation into which the project was launched.

By 2008, the world was experiencing the largest financial crisis since the Great Depression, almost a century ago. The agreed order upon which global prosperity had been built was eroding. The coveted financial institutions tasked with shepherding our collective financial order were collapsing under the weight of their own corruption, fraud, greed, and malpractice. Two decades of global prosperity following the end of the Cold War were grinding to an unceremonious halt as those in the trusted positions of power had corrupted the entire global financial framework to enrich themselves in the short term.

As families across the world saw their businesses fail, their houses repossessed, their jobs terminated, and their life savings wiped out by unaccountable bankers, credit rating agencies, mortgage brokers, and bureaucrats, Satoshi Nakamoto penned his 9-page proposal for one of the most radical reforms of global finance in centuries.

Bitcoin was indeed an idea whose time had come.

Hashcash

One of the primary ideas that Bitcoin utilises in its operation is based on a technology developed in 1997 by British cryptographer and computer Science PhD Adam Back.

The system was designed to prevent email spam by using cryptographic hashing of input data to require a small amount of computer processing power to send an email. The theory was that for an individual sending an email to a friend, this would be a trivial amount of computational power, and if it took an extra few seconds, that would be acceptable. However, a spammer sending millions of emails would require a large amount of computing power and electricity to send so many emails in a short space of time.

To understand how this works, we first need to understand how cryptographic hashing works:

In cryptographic hashing, we take an input piece of text and run it through a hashing algorithm to generate an output 'hash'. The 'hash' will be a long string of letters and numbers generated based upon the input we provided. The good thing is that the input can be as long or as short as we like, and the output 'hash' will always be a defined length. Equally, the output hash has no path back for someone to understand what the input text was; it is a one-way function that takes the input, runs it through an algorithm, and then produces a string of characters that nobody can reverse, but anyone who has the input text can verify.

To give a real world analogy to this process, consider the following:

Imagine your dear mother bakes you a beautiful birthday cake and hands it to you. You can see and enjoy the cake, but there's no way for you to take the cake apart and get the eggs, flour, and other ingredients back out of it. However, if your mum gives you the full recipe, you can bake the cake yourself, and the cake you get at the end will be identical to the one she made.

You can't get the eggs and flour back out of the end product, but if you have the recipe you can bake it yourself and verify that the recipe was indeed correct.

If we take a common cryptographic hashing function, known as MD5 hashing, we can try a few examples:

If we run the input: 'a' through the MD5 hashing algo, we get the output:

0cc175b9c0f1b6a831c399e269772661

If we run a longer string through the algorithm: 'It is 14:11 on the 23rd May 2023 and I am writing this from Batam, Indonesia, on a nice sunny day and enjoying a cold beer' we get the output:

98dbd426bb6bbaff0104eb046fdb0c59

Now, if we take that same input from above but change it slightly, and run it again through the hashing algorithm, we will get an entirely different hash.
If we simply take out the first comma in the input so that it now reads: 'It is 14:11 on the 23rd May 2023 and I am writing this from Batam Indonesia, on a nice sunny day and enjoying a cold beer' we get the output:

d92e0d1fa4c307f1676fdfa231e3b7c4

Now, if you search on Google for an MD5 hash generator, you can take the above input strings and check that the output hashes match exactly the hashes I was able to generate.

However, if i only give you an output hash string:

c36cf48ad139f6d33b936d89cf35379a

You're not going to be able to get my secret input string that I used to generate it.

In practice, a good way of storing passwords on many websites is to take a hash of the password and store that in a database.

That way, whenever you input your password into the website the website generates a hash of your password and checks it against the hash in the database.

If an attacker knows the hash of your password, there are some methods that hackers can use to attack this, for example a hacker could generate the hash of every word in a dictionary and then check your hash against that and if there is a match the hacker would know what your password is; the MD5 hash of the input 'password' is:

5f4dcc3b5aa765d61d8327deb882cf99

Googling that hash string will show a bunch of results that explain that it is the known hash value of the input 'password' because it is a common word and the hash of it is well known.

To mitigate this, some websites require you add special characters to your passwords such as uppercase and lowercase letters, numbers, and symbols, which are all good things to do but there are other methods we can take to obfuscate the input string from a known hash.

One common example is known as 'salting' the hash or adding a 'salt' to the input text. This is where before the input is put through the hashing algorithm, a known piece of text is added to it in order to change the resulting hash output.

For example if we take the word 'password' it would be very easy to reverse from the hash output as this is a very prominent word and many people have shared what the resulting hash is, so it's easy to reverse. But what if, before we hash the input string, we add our own piece of text to it so that the resulting hash will NOT be the same as the naked hash of the input text?

For example if we take the base input again of 'password' but we decide before we hash it we will add our own secret of '_~#Banana' so that the input text to be hashed is 'password_~#Banana' the output hash is:

6f52e18f403726b9424f609d446ba7d4

Attempting to reverse that is then not possible as nobody has publicly shared what the known hash of that bizarre input is, and crucially it changes the output hash string significantly different from the raw input of 'password' and no connection could be made.

This essentially forms the basis of the process that Hashcash outlined, but in a very unique and interesting way.

Under the Hashcash system in order to send an email the sender would have to provide a hash of the emails contents including the sender, recipient, and other meta data. The genius part of the system here, however, was that the output hash string must meet a fixed requirement in order to be allowed through.

So here we have a system using cryptographic hashing but not for passwords; in fact the entire input content is known - it is the content of the email - BUT the hash needs to meet a fixed requirement in order to get through the system, so how can we do that?

In order to do that the system makes use of this salting idea by having the sender add various arbitrary text to the input before it is hashed in order to generate a completely different output hash.

For example, the Hashcash system could say that in order to send an email I need to generate a hash of the email's contents, plus my salt, that ends in '00' in order to be allowed through the system.

To achieve this, the system uses a 'Number used once' or 'nonce' added to the end of the email input and changes that number over and over in order to generate new hashes until it finds one that fits the criteria of the system. I would simply hash '{email-contents}1', '{email-contents}32', '{email-contents}567' using either sequential numbers or random numbers, until I got an output hash string that ended in '00'

Once I find the right 'nonce' that, when added to my email contents, produces a hash output that ends in '00' I can pass the whole thing to the Hashcash system that simply runs a single hash - my email + my 'nonce' and can verify that it does indeed end in '00' and it sends my email.

The correct solution is very easy to verify, but to find the correct solution requires the sender to run multiple hashes over and over until they find one that matches. This asymmetry of difficulty is the key part and allows the verifier to check easily whilst the submitter has to do a lot of computational work.

What's more, the system can apply a 'difficulty adjustment' any time it chooses, by making it harder to more difficult for the submitter to find a valid matching hash. Simply by adjusting the number of characters that the hash has to match. For example instead of saying that the last 2 characters must be '00' the system could say the last 3 characters must be '000' increasing the difficulty and the cost/time that the submitter must pay in order to run more computational time to generate a hash that matches. Given that running a computer to crunch numbers takes time and electricity, this puts a real world cost on the person seeking to submit a valid hash string to the system and thereby acts as a real world cost incentive not to send spam emails.

All of these systems were adopted and adapted by Bitcoin and incorporated into the process by which bitcoins are mined, which we will explore in a later chapter.

Public-Key Cryptography

Another technology that Bitcoin makes heavy use of is that of public and private cryptographic key pairs. The way this works is a person is able to generate a pair of cryptographic keys that are linked to each other by an encryption algorithm. These are known as the Public and Private keys. Being joined together as they are through the encryption algorithm used to generate them the two keys can be used to either encode or decode messages sent to them in the following ways.

A message may be encrypted using the Public key, that may then ONLY be decrypted by the Private key.

A message encrypted using the Private key may ONLY be decrypted using the Public key

Extending the birthday cake analogy, imagine that the public and private keys are special tools. A cake made using the private key can be 'unmade' using the public key, and vice versa, but only if the correct key is used. For example a cake made using the private key can use the public key to get the eggs and flour back out of the cake; a cake made using the public key can have the eggs and flour taken out using the private key.

Both of these actions are then easily verified by any third party, though they would need the respective key to do so. Given the nature of the two keys, for the most part this is only then publicly possible using the Public key.

In principle then this is fairly straightforward, when generating a bitcoin wallet address a person generates a set of Public and Private keys that are connected via an encryption algorithm.

The Public key becomes your Bitcoin wallet address which can be shared publicly, and the Private key becomes effectively the keys or the password for that wallet.

If I have bitcoin in my wallet and I want to send it to you, I encrypt a message using my private key to say that I authorise moving 1 bitcoin from my wallet to your public key (Bitcoin wallet address).

The nodes and miners in the Bitcoin network can see the encrypted message and then use my public key (Bitcoin wallet address) to decode the message, which works since my private key and public key are linked.

Only someone in possession of my private key could have encrypted the message correctly so that it can be decoded with my public key, so the Bitcoin network accepts the transaction as valid because it was 'signed' by my private key.

Now the Bitcoin network collectively agrees to the transaction and updates the ledger to show the 1 bitcoin is now in your control.

When you wish to move the bitcoin from your control to another, you repeat the process by using your Private key to encode a message saying you wish to send the coins to another wallet (another public key), and the network can readily decode your message by using your public key (wallet address) as the key to decode the message.

Another, but less used, feature here is that you can also simply announce a message using your private key, and that can be decoded using your public key. For example if you wanted to announce that you are the owner of a wallet you could take your private key and encode a message saying 'Dan Clarke is the owner of this wallet on this date and time 23/05/2023 17:26' and then encode the message with your private key and publish it publicly, on your social media or wherever. Provided that you also post the wallet address (public key) to which you are referencing, then anyone can take that public key and decode the message and know that you have access to the private keys to that wallet in order to have encoded that message.

For the most part, however, these key pairs are simply used for sending and receiving bitcoin by authorising transactions to be sent (using private key and decrypted by your public key) or received (using public key and later sent using private key).

Guarding your private key then becomes vitally important, as anyone who has it can send your bitcoin to any other address.

Bit Gold

The closest technological idea to Bitcoin that existed before 2008 is certainly the idea of 'Bit Gold', a theoretical proposal outlined in 1998 by American computer scientist and cryptographer Nick Szabo.

Whilst the Bitcoin whitepaper does not reference Bit Gold by name, the Bitcoin protocol uses many of the same ideas outlined in Bit Gold and it is clear that whoever Satoshi Nakamoto was, he was certainly aware of Bit Gold.

Bit Gold remained a theoretical proposal that was never fully implemented in reality and some of the key functions were never explained in detail but the core concepts included:

Proof of Work: Utilising the system of forcing a user to hash their input strings over and over adding an arbitrary addition of text, until the resulting hash met the specified criteria - just as we explained above in the Hash Cash system. This required users to expend energy and time running computational tasks (hashing strings) until they found a hash that fit the required result - for example the hash must end with '00'

Chaining Transactions Together: In what is broadly understood to be the basis of the idea of a 'blockchain', Bit Gold proposed that all updates to the system (new coins, transactions, etc.) must reference and validate previous updates. This meant that the system would create a chain of updates with previous updates being validated and reinforced by new updates. For example a person running the system and using the Proof of Work system to create new Bit Gold would need to connect it to previous updates in the system, so that each new update would secure and validate the previous updates. Whilst the concept of 'blocks' was not described in the proposal, the chaining together of sequential updates was an important concept that ensured the system remained in sync and gave increasingly more confirmations of the validity of previous updates as the chain grew longer. If I ran the software and generated some Bit Gold by solving some computationally demanding hashing problem, then the next guy does the same but in his update he acknowledges and validates my update, then my update gains the security of that guy's update because his Proof of Work that he spent also validates my update, and so on, and so on.

Using a Decentralised Network: Importantly, the Bit Gold proposal outlined the idea of publishing all of the system updates to a system of 'nodes' (computers running the software) and having each node check and verify the update if it was valid or not.

This was possibly the most important idea that sets Bit Gold apart from other cryptographic projects or ideas and one could argue is the killer feature that underpins the Bitcoin network.

The decision to make the system decentralised removes the need for a centralised authority that is in the position to approve or disapprove any actions on the network and acts as both a single point of failure, but also of corruptibility and censorship.

In proposing Bit Gold, Szabo took great lengths to develop a system that had no single point of authority that could be stopped, corrupted, censored, or otherwise controlled. To understand the underlying genius in this system, we need to first take a step back and examine how traditional financial systems work.

If we take a traditional financial system and break it down into its parts and steps, we can get an understanding of how things typically work.

As I sit in a cafe here in Indonesia and drink an iced coffee, I get my bill and proceed to the cashier to pay:

1. I present my DBS credit card to the cashier who plugs it into his system and punches the price into a small computer. The computer reads the details from my card such as the card number, expiry date, etc. and then sends them, along with the bill amount, the cafe's merchant profile, etc. over the internet to the card processing company the cafe is using. (Point of authority 1)

2. The cafe's payment processing company then packages up this data and sends it to the Visa network (Point of Authority 2) for Visa to validate and process the transaction.

3. Since I am overseas in Indonesia and using a Singapore issued card, Visa then packages up this data and sends it to my bank in Singapore (Point of Authority 3) for them to verify and process the transaction.

4. My bank in Singapore receives the request and checks my account to see if I have sufficient credit to fulfill the transaction, and also checks if the transaction seems suspicious (large amount, strange location, etc.) and then if everything seems ok before sending an authorisation back to the Visa network

5. The Visa network then takes the authorisation and sends it back to the card payment processor that the cafe uses, and the cafe's machine notifies the cafe that the payment was successful.

6. At the end of the day, the payment processing system the cafe uses batches together all of the transactions from the day and sends them to the visa network.

7. The visa network collects all of the transactions from my Singapore bank and sends them to my bank

8. My bank transfers the money from them, to the Visa network

9. The Visa network sends the funds from Visa to the bank of the cafe.

This, frankly kafkaesque and drawn out process relies on 3 trusted parties to act correctly and creates 3 points of failure.

1. The cafe's bank has to be trusted to process my purchase

correctly, to not change the billed amount, not steal my card details, and to process the transaction honestly. It has the ability to simply reject the transaction without reason.

2. The Visa network is trusted to do the same.

3. My Singapore bank is trusted to do the same.

If any of these points fail because they are, for whatever reason, not working - the transaction fails.

Moreover, if any of these points decide not to authorise the transaction - for any reason whatsoever - the transaction fails. Worse still, any of these points could become corrupted and act incorrectly either through malicious intent or error, resulting in an incorrect transaction. The cafe's payment processor could overcharge or undercharge the bill, it could route it to someone else's account other than mine, it could make the payment to an account other than the cafe's, etc. My bank could overcharge, undercharge, or even charge the transaction to another customer of theirs, and the bank of the cafe could do the same on their receiving end.

The entire process relies on trusting third parties to act correctly at every step, in a system that is closed from public scrutiny as the entire process is conducted.

I could, of course, pay with cash; but this also does not remove the need for placing trust in a central authority. The cashier first has to trust me that the bank note I hand him is not counterfeit, he has to trust the Bank of Indonesia (Bank Indonesia) that the bank note will still be valid when he deposits it in his bank, and moreover that they haven't printed trillions of Rupiah in bank notes and therefore debased the value of the note before he is able to spend it.

In traditional finance, there is no method of payment that is possible without placing blind trust in some trusted third party acting as an authority in the system.

As we have seen in chapter one, central authorities in these systems are prone to failure through corruption, mismanagement, human error, and a multitude of other factors.

This is not to say that all central authorities and banks are bad and evil people, the overwhelming majority of them are good and honest and act with probity. However it is inherent in human nature to want to act in one's own best interests, even at times when that disadvantages others. Such is the tragedy of the commons.

The history of mankind is littered with examples of failings of those placed in positions of power and authority to tip the scales in their favour, it is as much a part of then human condition as is love, or grief, or laughter. We don't even need to look back so long in history to find examples of this; in chapter one we covered how bankers and other trusted figures sold unsuitable mortgages to people unable to sustain them, lining their pockets with commissions and bonuses, but ultimately leading to the 2008 financial crisis that destroyed the lives of many.

> *"All is clouded by desire: as fire by smoke, as a mirror by dust ...Through these it blinds the soul."*
> — C.J. Koch

Bit Gold in its proposed implementation outlined the basis of a radical system in which payments between parties can be made without requiring the trust of a third party.

The key point of this system is that rather than try to avoid the failings of individuals to act in their own self interest, even when that is to the detriment of others, but to utilise this in aggregate. Whilst an individual may be corruptible and act in their selfish personal interest, Bit Gold proposed a system that was essentially adversarial in nature in that each party would be best served acting in their own interest by acting in the agreed consensus and monitoring and rejecting any other party that attempted to break with the agreed consensus for their own benefit. This is achieved by building a system that is known as 'Byzantine Fault Tolerant' to detect and disregard anyone breaking with the agreed truth, and having multiple unrelated parties that all observe and report what that reality is, in order to detect anyone that is being dishonest.

Understanding this idea of Byzantine fault tolerance is another key point in understanding how Bitcoin works, so let's explore what it is and how it functions.

Byzantine Fault Tolerance: The name Byzantine Fault Tolerance comes from an interesting thought exercise known as the Byzantine Generals Problem. The names in the problem are not relevant, so in order to explain it let's take a more topical approach to this problem that doesn't involve esoterically named ancient empires.

Imagine the Ukrainian army have surrounded the city of Bakhmut in Eastern Ukraine, the Ukrainian army are camped out in 10 divisions around the city but are not connected to each other and Russian jamming has blocked all radio and internet communications so that each division of the Ukrainian army cannot simply radio or message the other divisions to confirm their plan.

Each Ukrainian division is headed by a General, and they all realise that in order to recapture the city they need to all attack at the same time; if a single division or couple of divisions chose to attack unilaterally, the Russian defences in Bakhmut would overwhelm them, but if they all attacked at the same time then victory would be assured. The pre-agreed plan was to attack at 20:00 on Friday, but it requires that each division make a simple choice to either 'Attack' or 'Hold', that is the agreement they all need to reach.

The problem however is that some of the generals may have been compromised by the Russians and may send false orders to other divisions in order to try and cause the attack to fail. Moreover, the lack of radio or internet means that the only way the generals can communicate with each other is by sending a messenger to run through the occupied areas and deliver a message to the other divisions. There is a small chance that messengers may be killed and not arrive, or be substantially delayed.

In this situation, we need to develop a system that can handle this tricky situation and still get a clear agreement between all of the generals to coordinate their attack. This is where the system of Byzantine Fault Tolerance is established.

Each general sends a messenger from his division to every other division with their decision to either 'Attack' or 'Hold', the loyal generals send a true message and the traitorous generals send a false message. In each case, the generals act in their best interest.
In this situation, each general understands that if they receive 6 or more messages from other divisions then that action is to be taken.

For example in this situation we may have 9 loyal generals and 1 traitor. The generals send their messengers and one of the other generals receives them.
Assuming one of the loyal generals' messengers gets killed, the recipient would then receive 8 valid messages, 1 false message, and 1 missing message.

8 x 'Attack'
1x 'Hold'
1x 'No message'

The other generals would receive messages in a similar pattern, possibly some receive 7x 'Attack' as two messengers were killed, or some may receive 9 x 'Attack' if the traitorous messenger is killed. However in all cases the generals would each receive 6 or more truthful messages of 'Attack' and any false message of 'Hold' can be detected as traitorous and disregarded.

The distributed generals are then able to reach a group consensus on truth, despite malicious actors attempting to lie, and despite the risk of messages being lost.

This is the basis of Byzantine Fault Tolerance as the faults in the system are understood and planned around.

This works by aligning the personal interests of each general and on the basis that, in aggregate, the number of traitors in the system is sufficiently greater than the number of traitors.

With the use of modern technology the risk of messages not arriving, or being intercepted can almost entirely be mitigated, but also the larger the number of parties in the system, the higher the likelihood of reaching a truthful consensus even in the event that a small number of messages fail or get corrupted.

Another simple modern world example of this would be to imagine a fleet of 50,000 automated cars that run around a city such as Singapore. Each of the cars constantly report their location and speed to every other car in the network and they all use this data to detect traffic jams or roadblocks and route around them to have more efficient journeys for their passengers.
If one of the cars in the system decides to report that a road is closed, because that car wants to keep the road clear so it can use it for itself to have quicker journeys, it could report false

data to all the other cars saying that the road is blocked or under heavy traffic.
The other cars in the system would have no incentive to collude in this lie and the cars that drove along that road just before and just after the malicious car would all report there to be no traffic or blocks on that road.
As a result, the system would identify the malicious car and reject its information.
The system works correctly with every party acting in its own best interest and is able to instantly detect a bad actor sending incorrect data to advantage itself.
Even if 100 cars were somehow able to collude to try and send incorrect data about the road, the remaining 49,900 cars that pass the road would send correct data and the colluding bad actors data would be rejected.
If the system was set to accept agreement only if 70% of cars agree, then the malicious acting cars would need to convince 35,000 cars to go along with its lie which would realistically be impractical to achieve.

The system is built to understand that each party acts in its own best interest and immediately detect those who try to cheat that system for their own benefit.

In the case of Bit Gold, and later Bitcoin, that use proof-of-work systems, the 'generals' from the Byzantine Generals Problem analogy are the miners, who solve complex hashing problems to add new blocks to the blockchain. These miners number in the many thousands, which means that for a malicious consensus to be reached, there would need to be a similarly large number of malicious miners acting in collusion. Given that miners (and nodes) are often anonymous and distributed across the globe, there's no practical way for them to collude on such a scale without detection.

B-Money

Another idea that predates Bitcoin and covers many of the same underlying concepts was outlined in 1998 by Chinese computer engineer and cryptographer Wei Dei.

The B-Money system operated broadly the same way as Bit-Gold in that it proposed to use Proof-of-Work as a means to generate virtual currency, and the use of a distributed database in which each person maintains a copy of the entire system and who owns what.
This is broadly understood as being the first proposal of a Distributed Ledger system where the records of who owns all of the currency in the system is stored on all of the nodes of the system.

B-Money also first introduced the idea of smart contracts that could be executed on the network by consensus of all of the parties.

As with Bit Gold, the proposal for B-Money remained theoretical and was never meaningfully implemented.

3

Who is/was Satoshi?

> *"Pour vivre heureux, vivons cachés."*
> — Jean de La Fontaine

Satoshi Nakamoto is the pseudonym used by the inventor of Bitcoin in publishing the whitepaper and subsequent emails and message board discussions. In the 15 years since, there has been much speculation as to the true identity of the person or persons behind the pseudonym, and whilst there are many potential candidates, the true identity of Satoshi Nakamoto remains unknown.

There are many reasons why the inventor of Bitcoin could have chosen to remain anonymous. In 2006, Arthur Budovsky, an American national, set up a parallel currency to the US Dollar for online payments. The system allowed users to purchase digital currency to use in online transactions and to buy or sell the digital currency. Arthur is currently serving a 20 year sentence in federal prison for his efforts. More recently, we have seen key figures targeted by law enforcement for their work in the digital currency space. Arthur Hayes, the founder of crypto exchange BitMEX served a 6 month detention and paid $10m in fines for violations of the Bank Secrecy Act. Sam Bankman-Fried, the founder of crypto exchange FTX was sentenced to 25 years in federal prison, and Do Kwon, the founder of Terra/Luna sits in a Montenegro prison facing a long stretch of time behind bars.

Whilst Bankman-Fried and Kwon are accused of many crimes of intentional mismanagement, Budovsky and Hayes essentially came up short with law enforcement for giving their users the ability to transact anonymously without submitting all of their personal particulars, something that is built into the very foundations of Bitcoin.

Aside from that, by being known, Satoshi would become a target of much attention from people who might not have the best of intentions. Critics could pore over their life to find any historical failing of which all humans are guilty and try to leverage that against the project to discredit it. Ex-wives or ex-girlfriends might be incentivised to come forward with horror stories - real or imagined - to discredit the inventor and the project.

Moreover, as an early user of Bitcoin, Satoshi is understood to control approximately one million bitcoins, which—depending on the current price of bitcoin—would place his personal net worth anywhere in the region of $30–70 billion. The past 15 years are littered with cases of criminals visiting violence upon bitcoin holders in order to relieve them of their wealth. A handful of cases from the last 5 years, in the US alone, show this is a very real and present issue.

In 2018, a man in New York City was robbed at gunpoint and forced to hand over his Bitcoin. The robbers made off with $1 million worth of Bitcoin.

In 2019, a man in Florida was kidnapped and tortured for his Bitcoin. The kidnappers made off with $2 million worth of Bitcoin.

In 2020, a man in California was robbed at gunpoint and forced to hand over his Bitcoin. The robbers made off with $1.5 million worth of Bitcoin.

In 2021, a man in Texas was robbed at gunpoint and forced to hand over his Bitcoin. The robbers made off with $1 million worth of Bitcoin.

In 2022, a man in Arizona was robbed at gunpoint and forced to hand over his Bitcoin. The robbers made off with $500,000 worth of Bitcoin.

Nonetheless, speculation remains rife as to the true identity of Satoshi Nakamoto, so let's look at what we do know and who the prime suspects are.

Circumstantial Evidence

By now, every single piece of information that Satoshi Nakamoto put out into the world has been pored over and analysed by thousands of people and institutions around the world. Every word, every grammatical mark or error, even down to the meta-data of when it was posted has been analysed and cross referenced with other bodies of work in order to try and unmask who the real Satoshi was. In a testament to Satoshi's brilliance, we remain in no meaningful way closer to understanding who he was today than we did when he launched the project.

What we do have are often conflicting data points and circumstantial evidence that often points in opposing directions as to who the person behind the mask is.

British English

Throughout the time Satoshi was posting updates about the project to the public message boards and emailing correspondence with other early adopters, it was noted that, whoever they were, they wrote using British English spelling. Posts and updates would use the word 'colour' rather than the American spelling of 'color', 'honour' rather than 'honor', 'realise' rather than 'realize', as well as using phrases and expressions that are common in British English but not found in American English—for example, using the word 'flat' rather than 'apartment', or 'maths' over the preferred American term 'math', and in perhaps the clearest example, referring to something as 'bloody hard'.

This could imply that Satoshi was British, or from a common-

wealth country that uses British English, such as Australia, New Zealand, India, Singapore, etc.
It could equally be an intentional red herring used to throw analysts off of his true origin.

UK Timezone

Researchers at the University of Nicosia in Cyprus analysed the posting times of over 500 posts made by Satoshi to the public messaging board 'Bitcoin Talk' and found the following insights.

The vast majority of posts were made between 08:00 and 18:00 UK time

The number and frequency of posts declined during the months of summer time in the UK - with the implication that Satoshi took some downtime during the summer

This circumstantial evidence would point towards the idea that Satoshi was likely living in the UK at the time he developed Bitcoin.

Genesis Block Inscription

Another indication that Satoshi was living in the UK at the time of its initial development is the message that Satoshi encoded into the first ever block on the Bitcoin blockchain. Whenever a new block is added to the Bitcoin blockchain through the Proof-of-Work system there is a small space for the creator to add a small text message into the block. On the 3rd January 2009, Satoshi created the first block of the Bitcoin chain—also known as the 'Genesis Block'—and in the space for a message, wrote:

> *"The Times 03/Jan/2009 Chancellor on brink of second bailout for banks."*
> — Satoshi Nakamoto

This references the headline found on the front page of the British newspaper 'The Times' that day. Whilst 'The Times' already had a website version of their newspaper in 2009 it seems somewhat unlikely that a person outside of the UK would have chosen the headline from a British newspaper to permanently etch into the foundation of the Bitcoin chain. Unless, again, this was a clever act of misdirection.

Writing Analysis

In 2016, a team of researchers at the University of California, Berkeley, used stylometry to analyse the entire known body of writing that Satoshi had ever written and compare it against people they suspected to be Satoshi. Whilst this is not a perfect science, the results of the analysis showed similarities with several of the people suspected to be Satoshi, including Hal Finney, and Dorian Nakamoto, but in particular it found a stronger correlation with that of Nick Szabo, noting that the sentence structures of both were very similar in the words they used, the way they structured their sentences, and the way they used punctuation. The researchers concluded at the time that the similarities were 'statistically significant' and opined that they were, in their opinion, too close to be a coincidence.

Possible Suspects

As I mentioned earlier in this chapter, there remains no consensus as to the real identity of Satoshi Nakamoto and evidence is often conflicting. The following people have all been, at various times, suspected of being Satosh and have all issued denials to that accusation, with the exception of Craig Wright who conversely has claimed to be Satoshi but presented much discredited and fraudulent evidence and been involved in numerous lawsuits that have failed to validate his claim. Anyone considered credible as being Satoshi has denied it. Conversely, those claiming to be Satoshi have not been found credible.

Nick Szabo

One of the primary individuals frequently suspected of being behind the name Satoshi Nakamoto is Nick Szabo. As we mentioned in the previous chapter, Szabo introduced many of the technological ideas that Bitcoin is built on top of in his 1998 proposal for Bit-Gold. It is clear that whoever Satoshi was, he was certainly very familiar with Szabo's work and held a deep understanding of it. In addition, the 2016 analysis of Satoshi's writing found strong similarities between the style of Szabo's writing and that used by Satoshi; however, Szabo was known to be living in the US at the time of Satoshi's posts and writes in American English.

For his part, Szabo has constantly denied having any connection to the founding of Bitcoin and has denied being Satoshi on several occasions, stating in a 2014 email to financial author Dominic Frisby:

> *"I'm afraid you got it wrong doxing me as Satoshi, but I'm used to it"*

Hal Finney

Another leading candidate that is often suspected of being Satoshi is another American computer scientist and engineer, Hal Finney.

Finney is regarded as the first person to interact with the Bitcoin protocol and run the software himself, after Satoshi. Finney was among the first people to receive bitcoin directly from Satoshi and wrote a blog post about it in 2010 that helped the idea get significant attention.

On the 11th of June 2009, Finney tweeted from his public Twitter account, a now infamous tweet in the Bitcoin community, that said simply:

> *"Running bitcoin"*

Sadly, Finney passed away in August 2014 following a long illness with amyotrophic lateral sclerosis (ALS). As his condition worsened, Finney was unable to engage in much correspondence; however, he did issue a robust denial of the allegation in an email to an investigative journalist in early 2014:

> *"As for your suspicion that I either am or at least helped Satoshi, I'm flattered but I deny categorically these allegations. I don't know what more I can say."*

However, some other circumstantial evidence was uncovered by those investigating the identity of Bitcoin's founding father.

Firstly, that Finney passed away could well explain why Satoshi has never returned publicly to the project, despite his personal stash of bitcoins being worth over $70 Billion USD at its most recent peak. All things aside, it would take a lot of commitment to anonymity to turn your back on an amount of money that would instantly make you one of the wealthiest people in the world, yet Satoshi has not moved a single penny in many years and the wallets known to be associated with him sit dormant. Either Satoshi is indeed dead, or has lost the keys to the wallet, or simply values his privacy much more than most.

Another incredibly interesting twist of fate in this story of

Satoshi and Finney came to light in 2014 when Newsweek uncovered a man by the name of Dorian Satoshi Nakamoto.

Dorian, who went by his birth name of Satoshi, grew up and went to school in the neighbouring city to Finney in the late 60s and early 70s, and the pair lived just over a mile and a half apart from each other. Dorian was a keen computer scientist and advocate of digital privacy that went on to build a career in computer science and cryptography.
Perhaps the fact that the only computer scientist in the western world named Satoshi Nakamoto lived a mile and a half from Hal Finney in a Californian suburb is just a coincidence. Perhaps it isn't.

Dorian Nakamoto

Dorian S. Nakamoto is a Japanese-American computer scientist, cryptographer, and something of a social recluse, who was identified in 2014 by Newsweek magazine as being the founder of bitcoin. He is perhaps the most common face that has been used in media depictions of Satoshi, though use of his photo has faded in recent years. The photographs of a bewildered-looking, bespectacled Japanese man add a touch of irony when placed alongside stories of Bitcoin.
Newsweek investigative journalists scoured the US for people with the name Satoshi Nakamoto and then attempted to filter them until they found the person they most likely felt could be the founder of Bitcoin. Dorian was born 'Satoshi Nakamoto' and went by that name until the age of 23 when he legally changed it to 'Dorian Prentice Satoshi Nakamoto'.

Interestingly, Dorian remains a very private and reclusive man that typically shies from any kind of media engagement, which means the little that is known about him is mostly pieced together from those close to him. What is known is that Dorian spent most of his career working with US defence contracting firms working on secured communication technologies, which would almost certainly be using implementations of cryptography. Almost all of this work remains heavily classified which means that Dorian would not be able to talk about it, even if he had the inclination to. However this led to some ambiguity when the Newsweek reported doorstepped Dorian at his house in California in 2014 and asked him about the Bitcoin protocol.

> *"I am no longer involved in that and I cannot discuss it," he says, dismissing all further queries with a swat of his left hand. "It's been turned over to other people. They are in charge of it now. I no longer have any connection."*

Whilst Dorian would later claim he had no idea what Bitcoin was, and was referring to his prior classified military work, this tacit acknowledgment that he had been the founder of Bitcoin set off something of a media frenzy at the time.

Whilst there is some evidence that points to connect Dorian to the founder of Bitcoin, there is also evidence that would equally point to the contrary.

Throughout the 1990s, Dorian struggled to find work and fell behind on mortgage payments, he also lived in a modest home and seemed to genuinely be unaware of what Bitcoin was or how it worked when he later spoke with people familiar with Bitcoin, indeed in an interview with Associated Press shortly after the Newseek article, it was reported that Dorian:

> *"called the technology 'bitcom' [as he was] still unfamiliar with the term".*

Dorian also said that he stopped having an internet connection in his house in 2013 due to financial hardship he was facing - during a time when the founder of Bitcoin was sitting on almost half a billion dollars worth of bitcoin.

For his part, Dorian hired a lawyer and issued a strong and clear statement:

> *"I did not create, invent or otherwise work on bitcoin. I unconditionally deny the Newsweek report,"*

The Bitcoin community crowd sourced a fundraiser for Dorian and donated over 47 bitcoin, worth around $23,000 at the time.

Dave Kleiman

Dave Kleiman was an American computer forensics specialist and keen cryptographer that was an active member of the cryptography mailing list 'Metzdowd Cryptography' to which Satoshi introduced the initial Bitcoin whitepaper in 2008.

Kleiman was an accomplished computer scientist and cryptographer and known to be an early adopter of Bitcoin. But there is little by way of evidence to suggest that Kleiman was the original founder of the project.

The main basis of speculation that Kleiman was involved in the creation of Bitcoin comes from another person suspected of being Satoshi, Australian computer scientist Craig Wright, who claims that Kleiman helped him invent Bitcoin.

Kleiman passed away in 2013, having never claimed to be Satoshi nor having faced that allegation in any known meaningful way that is known.

Adam Back

Adam Back is a British leading cryptography consultant and computer scientist that introduced the idea of the Hashcash protocol in 1997. The Hashcash system laid the basis for the 'Proof of Work' system which was built upon by Bit-Gold and B-Money, and ultimately Bitcoin.

Back first publicly came to the Bitcoin community in 2013 when he joined the popular Bitcoin Talk message board that Satoshi had been a frequent contributor to.

Back currently remains in the Bitcoin space in a number of roles, including as a founding member and CEO of 'Blockstream', a Bitcoin services company that has led many important developments in the space.

There is little credible evidence to suggest that Back is Satoshi, and for his part he has denied it. In a May 2020 tweet, he said:

> *"I am not Satoshi despite recent video / reddit claiming so. some factors & timing may look suspicious in hindsight; coincidence & facts are untidy."*

Craig Wright

Craig Steven Wright is an Australian convicted criminal, computer scientist, that has repeatedly claimed to be Satoshi Nakamoto.

Prior to Bitcoin, Wright was convicted of Contempt of Court in 2004 in Australia and sentenced to 28 days in jail. He appealed the decision in 2005 and lost, before appealing it to the high court in 2006 where he also lost.

In December 2015, Wired and Gizmodo magazines both published articles in which they claimed their investigations had led them to believe that Satoshi Nakamoto was Craig Wright. This was based on evidence Wright submitted to them, including signing of emails using a cryptographic signature method known as PGP.
Cryptography experts immediately began to question this, noting that:

1. The PGP keys given by Wright as evidence of being Satoshi were easily forged and indeed appeared to have been forged using technology that did not exist in 2008 - when Wright claims they were created.

2. Wright claimed to have publicly posted the keys for verification on his blog in 2008 - however existing cached copies of the blog on other platforms show that they keys were added to the blog post some time after 2013

In May 2016 Wright published a blog article in which he claimed to be the creator of Bitcoin, Satoshi Nakamoto and included with it a block of text that he claimed was a famous speech, encrypted with the private key that Satoshi had used to send bitcoin in the 9th ever block that had been mined.

If true, this would be strong evidence as to get the valid hash out would require the private key and only Satoshi should have that. Wright shared an output that it was then possible to check if it really had been signed with the key Satoshi used in the 9th block, but it was NOT possible to use the public key to decode the input contents. Wright presented this along with his blog saying that he had encrypted a long string of text - a speech from Jean-Paul Sartre.

The output from this was, he claimed, his text encrypted with Satoshi's key and produced an output that the public could then check if it had been signed with Satoshi's key.

The output that Wright shared was checked - it was indeed 100% signed with Satoshis key that was used in the 9th Block.

However it was quickly found that this was, again, fraudulent and Wright had simply taken a signed hash from the 248th block (which is public) in which Satoshi HAD sent coins using the same private key as used in the 9th Block.
The transaction in the 248th block contained a signed message by Satoshi using the same key as in the 9th block and the known instructions - 'move x bitcoin to wallet y'.

The community was able to detect that the signed message Wright had shared was identical to a genuine message that had been signed by the Satoshi keys, but the input text of the message was not some quote that Wright had said, but was a historical bitcoin transaction. The possibility of this happening coincidentally are essentially trillions to one. The only explanation of this, experts conclude, can be intentional fraud. The blog post was subsequently taken down and deleted from Wrights blog.

Wright has subsequently claimed ownership of many wallets that were used in the early days of Bitcoin and contain billions of dollars of bitcoin. In recent years, people have signed messages using the keys to some of these wallets including with signed messages such as:

> *"Craig Steven Wright is a liar and a fraud. He doesn't have the keys used to sign this message."*

Wright has been further involved in numerous legal suits in recent years regarding his claim to be Satoshi. Wright was sued by Ira Kleiman, the brother of Dave Kleiman, in which intermediate rulings for:

> *"willful and bad faith pattern of obstructive behavior, including submitting incomplete or deceptive pleadings, filing a false declaration, knowingly producing a fraudulent trust document, and giving perjurious testimony at the evidentiary hearing,"*

Wright has also sued prominent critics, leading to libel lawsuits in Norway and the United Kingdom, with the Norwegian case finding against Wright, and the British case Judge surmising that he

> *"found Dr Wright not to be a witness of truth,"*

Who had put forward a:

> *"deliberately false case"*

In a subsequent case in May 2024 following a long series of legal cases, Craig Wright was found by the High Court of England and Wales to have been dishonest in his claims to be Satoshi Nakamoto and to have have lied consistently to the court in his attempts to assert his claim.

As part of the findings, the High Court demanded the following text be posted to Wrights website and social media accounts:

> *LEGAL NOTICE:*
> *DR CRAIG STEVEN WRIGHT IS NOT SATOSHI NAKAMOTO*
>
> *On 20 May 2024, Dr Craig Steven Wright was found by the High Court of England and Wales to have been dishonest in his claims to have been the person behind the pseudonym Satoshi Nakamoto (the creator of Bitcoin).*
>
> *The Court found that Dr Wright "lied to the Court extensively and repeatedly" in his evidence and that he attempted to create a false narrative by forging documents "on a grand scale" and presenting them in evidence. Overall, "all his lies and forged documents were in support of his biggest lie: his claim to be Satoshi Nakamoto." In advancing his false claim to be Satoshi through multiple*

legal actions, Dr Wright committed "a most serious abuse" of the process of the courts of the UK, Norway and the USA. The High Court formally declared as follows:

First, that Dr Wright is not the author of the Bitcoin White Paper.

Second, Dr Wright is not the owner of the copyright in the Bitcoin White Paper.

Third, Dr Wright is not the person who adopted or operated under the pseudonym Satoshi Nakamoto in the period between 2008 and 2011.

Fourth, Dr Wright is not the person who created the Bitcoin system.

Fifth, Dr Wright is not the author of the initial versions of the Bitcoin Software.

The full judgment, and its appendix detailing various forged documents created by Dr Wright, is accessible at the following URL: https://www.judiciary.uk/judgments/copa-v-wright/.

Dr Wright has been ordered not to commence any legal proceedings based on his false claims (by claim or counterclaim) or procure any other person to do so. He has also been ordered not to threaten any such proceedings (explicitly or implicitly) or procure any other person to do

> *so.*

Wright continues to claim he is Satoshi Nakamoto.

4

How Bitcoin Works

> *"Tick tock, next block"*
> — Satoshi Nakamoto

In the previous chapters, we covered much of the historical and theoretical background behind Bitcoin, but now it's time to roll up our sleeves and take a dive into how Bitcoin works in its real-world application.

As we covered earlier, Bitcoin was launched on 31st October 2008 with the publication of the whitepaper, which outlined the core principles of Bitcoin and how the system would work and operate. At nine pages long, it's certainly worth a read, as it explains the basis of how the network operates and covers the Bitcoin mining process, the long-term monetary policy of the network, and more.

So let's take a step back for a moment and try to understand what the Bitcoin network is at a very high level, before we pick apart the individual components for more detailed explanation.

Essentially, the Bitcoin network is a collection of computers around the world that all run the same software and each keep a copy of the database stored on their own devices. Another set of computers is running 24/7, trying to solve complicated hashing functions. Every 10 minutes, a computer solves the problem and gets to add a new update to the database, and is rewarded with some newly issued bitcoin for their troubles. All of the computers on the system check each other to make sure they are all recording the updates to the database in the right way, and each update to the database just updates the balances of the users in the database.

For example, if we have 3 players Tom, Dick, and Harry.

Tom owns 10 bitcoin.
Dick owns 0 bitcoin.
Harry owns 0 bitcoin.

The shared database on all of the computers around the world records this data, and all agree on it to be true.

Tom decides to send 5 bitcoin to Dick, so he publishes a message to the network saying that he wants to move 5 bitcoin from his wallet to Dick's, and signs the message using his private key so that everyone can be sure it's really him.

Meanwhile, Harry is trying to solve the hashing problem on his computer so that he can be the one chosen to update the database. Harry sees the message from Tom to send 5 bitcoin to Dick and checks that it has been properly signed using Tom's public key. Harry takes this message and packages it with other similar messages and gets ready to update the shared database with all these updates.

Harry is lucky, and his computer finds the right solution to the hashing problem, and he is able to broadcast an update to the database—including the fact that Tom sent 5 bitcoin to Dick.

To reward Harry for this work, the system issues him 2 bitcoin that are brand newly created.

Everyone on the network sees all of this, and agrees to update their version of the shared database.

The shared database now says:

Tom: 5 bitcoin
Dick: 5 bitcoin
Harry: 2 bitcoin

The system is constantly updating every 10 minutes as people choose to move their bitcoin between each other, and all of the computers in the system see the valid updates and agree to them.

How this works is similar in a way to traditional banking. Your bank has a database with all its customers' names in it and the dollar balances in those accounts. Every time you send or receive money, the bank just updates its database.

The difference in Bitcoin is that instead of that database being controlled by a single party, and hidden from the public, the database is controlled by everyone, and is 100% public.

This is possible because it uses blockchain technology, and everyone is able to agree on the correct state of the database because of the Byzantine Fault Tolerance we covered in the previous chapters.

Blockchain Technology

As we mentioned above, at its core, Bitcoin is simply a shared database that lists every user in the system and how many bitcoin they own. That, essentially, is it.

So what is a blockchain, and how does it work?

Each of the updates to the database is packaged into a group of data known as a 'block', which has a limited size—up to a maximum of 1 MB for the base size, or approximately 4 MB with SegWit transactions due to the block weight limit. These 'blocks' have to reference the previous 'block' that was pushed out to the system. In doing so, it creates a 'chain' of 'blocks' with each new block being connected to the one behind it.

In Bitcoin, around every 10 minutes, a new block is created, and miners (like Harry in the above example) fill up their block with as many transactions as they can and then race each other to try and be the first to solve the hashing problem and be allowed to add their block as the next update in the chain. All of the other computers in the network see this update, agree that it is valid, and update their own copies of the blockchain, which updates the balances for anyone that sent or received bitcoin in the most recent block of updates.

How this works in reality is that users around the world publish their wish to send a Bitcoin transaction, and how much of a fee they are willing to pay for that transaction to be added to the system in the next block. All of these pending transactions are published to the network, and miners pick up the greatest number of transactions that they can fit into the limited block size, prioritising those transactions that are willing to pay a higher fee.
Once the miner has a block filled with transactions, it hopes that it hits the right solution to the hashing problem and gets granted the permission to push its block as the next update in the chain.

The reason this system works is because of the number of people in the system, and that they have the incentive to act correctly. It also makes it practically impossible for anyone to try and cheat the system or change the database incorrectly.

The problem with digital currencies previously was always the issue of what is known as the 'Double Spend Problem', which is a very intuitive problem to understand. If I have a picture on my computer and I send it to you, the original stays on my computer, and I can send it to someone else. The problem there is that if the image, or whatever file it is, was digital currency, then the system wouldn't work as anyone could spend the same currency many times.

The blockchain solves this issue because the agreed status of the network is distributed over many thousands of computers around the world, with people willingly choosing to run the software and keep the network running correctly. If I took my own computer and tried to say to the network that I had 1,000 bitcoin, the other players in the network would see that this is not true and simply reject me from the network. If another player decided to claim they had another 1,000 bitcoin in their wallet, my system would reject them from the network.

The entire Bitcoin system is absolutely, entirely, adversarial in nature and operates on the understanding that nobody can be trusted, at all, ever. You can imagine it like a huge Mexican stand-off where every player in the game is holding a gun to every other player's head; if anyone tries to cheat, they are simply removed from the system. In the case of miners, if they act maliciously and add a block with incorrect data, the system would view the block as invalid, and other miners would attempt to mine a new block in its place. Given that it takes a lot of electricity to run the computers to solve the hashing problem to create a block, this means the miner would take a substantial financial loss by trying to cheat. The electricity and equipment bills would still need to be paid, but they would not get the new bitcoin as a reward for mining a new and valid block.

Mining Bitcoin

A key area that gets a lot of attention in the media is the idea of 'Bitcoin Mining' and the societal and environmental issues this potentially causes. We covered the basic idea of the Proof-of-

Work system in previous chapters and touched on how it works in Bitcoin. The process of bitcoin mining involves miners taking pending transactions and packing them together into a block. They then run that data, along with an arbitrary string called a 'nonce', through a hash function to generate a hash output and check if that hash output meets the criteria outlined by the Bitcoin system to be accepted. In return, the miner is awarded some freshly issued new bitcoin and gets the transaction fees that everyone paid to have their transaction included in his block.

The cost to buy the equipment plus the electricity to run the miners are the miners' costs, and the bitcoin they get is their reward. Provided the miner thinks they can make more in bitcoin than they pay in costs, they will run their hardware to mine bitcoin—that is just someone acting in their own best interest. Given this, others will also want to mine Bitcoin by running their own computers and hardware, and so healthy market competition is born. Over time more parties join and mine bitcoin and the market becomes broad and competitive. Some miners mine using large warehouses of complicated computer parts, some people run computers in their house to mine Bitcoin, and everything in between.

The huge energy expended to mine Bitcoin is what gives it its security. The other rational actors that are mining have no incentive to stop. This means that if you want to add a block to the blockchain, you are going to be competing with them to try and solve the hashing problem for the next block before anyone else does. With each new block in the chain, the previous block becomes more secure as any attacker has yet another block they would have to solve the hashing problem for, which is why many places make you wait until your transaction has 3-6 blocks mined after it before crediting your account.

Some miners mine directly using their hardware and simply try to find the right solution for the hashing problem for the next block, but many instead pool their resources in what is known as a 'mining pool'. In a mining pool, anyone can add their hardware to the team and have their computer try to solve the hashing problem. If the team gets a winning answer and the team is able to process the block then the reward is shared out equally among the members, depending on how much power they contributed.

Bitcoin's Blockchain

Since the invention of Bitcoin, there have been many new blockchains that have been developed with various features and changes. Later cryptocurrency projects such as Ethereum have faster chains, others have bigger sized blocks, and some do away with the mining process altogether.

But let us look at some of the important key features of the Bitcoin blockchain that make it work and how they all function together in harmony to keep the chain moving along in the right way.

Block Time

The first thing we need to consider is how often a new update can be added to the chain. This is an issue that we call the 'block time' as it is the time in between blocks.

Bitcoin has a block time of around 10 minutes—that is to say, a new block is added to the chain every 10 minutes, and new transactions are carried out. But how does the system keep the time so elegantly?

The reality is that blocks do average a time of 10 minutes per block but it's not uncommon to have blocks less than a minute after each other, or to go a period of an hour without a new block being added to the chain. This is because a new block is added whenever a miner is able to solve the hashing problem in the correct format and the system verifies it as correct.
Given that this system of guessing at the problem is random it leads to times when blocks get mined much quicker, or slower, than the 10 minute target.
Moreover, as the system grows and bitcoins become more valuable, there is a financial incentive to add more computing power to the system in order to try and solve the hashing problems quicker and get rewarded with new bitcoins. All of this needs to be considered and mitigated to build a system where even the random guessing of solutions to the hashing problems can average out at a new block of updates every 10 minutes.

To solve this, the Bitcoin blockchain constantly changes how difficult the hashing problem is to solve. Every 2,016 blocks - which should be around 14 days - the system looks at the

previous 2,016 blocks and checks if they were produced at an average rate of 10 minutes.
If the blocks were produced too quickly—because the hashing problem was being solved too quickly—then the difficulty of the hashing problem is increased; if the blocks were too slow, the difficulty is reduced. A harder problem will require more guesses and an easier problem will require fewer, so this way the network checks every 14 days and self adjusts to keep things on the right track and blocks added to the chain every 10 minutes.

But why 10 minutes? If we sped up the rate at which blocks are added then we could increase the capacity of the network and get more transactions flowing on the system, however with all changes this comes with consequences. The Bitcoin chain is global and requires thousands of computers around the world to all agree upon the state of the network and that takes a little time for the full message of any update to get around the world, through everyones internet connections, and to their computers - and for their computers to validate the updates and save it. By having a 10-minute time between blocks, this is ample time for everyone around the world to do this, even if they have a weak internet connection.

If the block time was reduced to, for example, 1 minute then the random nature of the solving of the hashing problem would mean that some blocks get added mere seconds after the previous one, possibly several blocks in a row. This would be problematic for the entire network to receive, validate, and save all of these updates so quickly. The key feature of the Bitcoin blockchain is to avoid mistakes and to lock each new addition to the chain as a permanent update. Having a block time of 10 minutes feels like the right balance between being quick enough to be functional, but slow enough to reduce the risk of the network becoming meaningfully out of sync with parts of itself.

Block Size

Another area that is potentially open to change is the size limit of each new block that is added to the chain. If the size limit were bigger then, again, we could fit in more transactions per block and increase the amount of transactions that can occur on the network which should lead to more adoption. However, this again comes with consequences. Everyone running the Bitcoin software on their computer - the nodes - has to download the entire content of the blockchain and keep a stored copy of it. As of June 2023, the combined total of all of that data is just shy of 500 gigabytes. That is substantial, but we have to remember that it covers every single use of Bitcoin for the last 14 years, all the way back to Satoshi's first ever block. The entire history of Bitcoin, and it would all fit on an external hard drive you can pick up for $30 from Amazon - there is an inherent beauty in this accessibility.

Increasing the size of blocks would mean that the size of the blockchain data would balloon, and it would quickly become impractical for people to run the system on their computers or dedicated home devices. This would mean the system could only really be run on large datacentres. This would drastically reduce the decentralisation of the system.

You see, with every potential upgrade there is often a negative to consider, and Satoshi seems to have chosen block times and sizes that meet these two in the middle.

Nakamoto Consensus

Given the distributed nature of all of the nodes and miners in Bitcoin, the system also needs to find a method for resolving discrepancies that may arise due to the network falling out of sync. As we mentioned above, new blocks have to be sent to all the participants of the network for them to receive, validate, and add to their systems - but what if during the time that takes to process, a different miner solves the same hashing problem and tries to add their own block instead?

In this case we have 2 miners, Miner A solves the hashing problem and adds a block to the chain and sends that out to all of the nodes to verify. However, before that update reaches the entire network, Miner B also solves the same hashing problem and adds a block to the chain at the same point in the chain as Miner A and sends that out to the entire network.
The delay in the network updating, plus the random guessing nature of the hashing problem makes this a possibility, but one for which Satoshi had a proposed solution that is known as the 'Nakamoto Consensus'.

In our above example, both miners have solved the hashing problem and added blocks to the chain and both are valid, but the system cant have two alternate blocks sitting in the same place on the chain. Firstly, who would get the new bitcoin that are issued as a reward? But also the transactions in one block would likely be different from the transactions in the other, so there would be no agreement on which transactions happened. The system can only function if it agrees to pick only one of these two valid blocks and everyone needs to agree on which one it is, without any central authority to make the decision. In this case, it falls to the subsequent miners which block they choose to add their new block to when they solve the next hashing problem. Each new block has to reference the previous block and can only reference one block, so the next miner will have to make a decision which one to reference. Even if the next block gets added to the chain that Miner A mined, Miner B could still continue to mine and reference his block and attempt to keep going there, however the Nakamoto Consensus states that whichever of the two chains is longer is the valid one. So, unless Miner B was able to mine many blocks quickly and add blocks to his split chain faster than the rest of the network was adding blocks to the other chain, then all of his resources spent on mining blocks on his chain would be wasted.

This then encourages Miner B to give up chasing his split chain, accept the bad luck of missing out on one block, and get back to work mining for blocks on the main chain again.

Supply Cap & Halving

Another feature that is hardcoded into the Bitcoin protocol is both the limit on the number of bitcoin that there ever will be, and the rate at which those new coins are issued. What makes this different from fiat currencies such as the US Dollar or British Pound is that this hard limit is known and verifiable, which means there can be no inflation of the money supply as there is in fiat currencies. As we saw in the first chapter, at moments of crisis history is littered with authorities inflating their money supply away. The closest example of this in the real world would be gold, in fact Bitcoin is also sometimes referred to as 'Digital Gold' however, the exact rate at which new gold is found, and how much there will ever be, cannot be known with certainty - unlike with Bitcoin.

The network produces new bitcoin every time a new block is added to the chain, with the new bitcoin coming into existence immediately and being awarded to the miner that solved the hashing problem correctly. This is known as the 'block reward' and is added into the block in a special transaction known as the 'coinbase' - Yes, like the company.

Now, in another well-thought-out move, the Bitcoin protocol outlined in the whitepaper that this reward for solving the hashing problem and adding a new block to the chain would start out at 50 bitcoin per block but would cut in half every 210,000 blocks—roughly every four years—in a process known as the 'halving'.

As of October 2024, the block reward paid out to miners for adding a block to the chain is currently 3.125 bitcoin, with the reward reduction cut earlier this year. The system is currently around three and a half away from the next halving where that reward will be cut to 1.5625 bitcoin per new block.

This system has two great features, firstly the number of bitcoin available at any point in the future can be calculated exactly, following the known formula, but also this reduction in the rate of new bitcoin being added to the system creates increased scarcity in the amount of bitcoin available. Historically these halving cycles have been big events in the Bitcoin community and the subsequent reduction in bitcoin supply has - many speculate - been a key driver in the subsequent price rises of bitcoin. This would seem to make logical sense if we assume that the demand for bitcoin is either stable or increasing - and the supply of bitcoin is halved - the economic laws of supply and demand would dictate that prices have to rise. It is also observable that bitcoin tends to go through price cycles that have historically been 4 years long, peaking in the year after the halving and bottoming out in the year before it - though it remains to be seen if this will continue.

The known absolute supply cap and predictable rate of issuance of bitcoin make the Bitcoin system a very 'hard' money, in the Austrian economics sense. There will only ever be 21 million bitcoin in the world, and the last ones won't be issued for over 120 years. In the last 14 years since Bitcoin started, already more than 90% of the supply has been issued, the remaining 2 million or so bitcoin will be issued increasingly slowly, every 10 minutes until some day in 2140.

UTXOs

Finally, in understanding how the Bitcoin blockchain works, we need to cover how the system handles the actual bits that we call the bitcoins themselves. In the Bitcoin protocol, all bitcoins are issued when a new block is added to the chain by whoever solved the hashing problem to allow them to add the block—

the entities we call miners. The system issues new bitcoin to the miners as a reward and the system carries on. But what *are* bitcoin?

There's no easy way to say this, so, there kind of isn't really any such thing as a bitcoin. What we broadly call bitcoins are actually just a bunch of what the system calls 'Unspent Transaction Outputs' or UTXOs. A UTXO is essentially just a receipt that says you received X bitcoin and haven't spent them yet - hence the name 'unspent'. If we think back to when we explored what money was, we discussed that the money in your wallet is never yours, it's just your turn to spend it; this is a similar way you could think of UTXOs - you have them, in this case you do 'own' them, and when its your turn you can spend them.

The other thing to know about UTXOs is that they can be broken up into smaller parts, or added together to form bigger parts. If I had mined an early block on the chain the system would have issued me a UTXO for 50 bitcoin. If I then wanted to send 2 bitcoin to my friend, Ayu, the Bitcoin network would take the UTXO for 50 bitcoin and break it into 2 new UTXOs, one for 2 bitcoin that it would send to Ayu, and one for 48 bitcoin that it would send back to me. Ayu then has a UTXO for 2 bitcoin that she can send by signing a message with her private key, and I have a UTXO for 48 bitcoin that I can send on with my private key.

If Ayu then gets 2 more bitcoin from 4 other people, she then has 5 UTXOs of 2 bitcoin each in her bitcoin wallet. Suppose she wants to send 9 bitcoin to someone, she would then combine all 5 of her UTXOs and the system will create 2 new UTXOs, one of

1 bitcoin back to Ayu and one for 9 bitcoin that gets sent to the recipient.

The entire system of people moving bitcoin is simply this: it is UTXOs being assigned to another bitcoin wallet address in the system. UTXOs being added together or broken into smaller parts. If you send bitcoin to someone, your wallet will gather up however many UTXOs it needs to be above the amount you intend to send, then send them to the system to break down into the amount the recipient gets, and your change back as a new UTXO.

Holding bitcoin then simply means that you hold the private key that allows you to transfer UTXOs to the value of x bitcoin. If you hold the private key to be able to move a total of UTXOs worth 50 bitcoin - you hold 50 bitcoin. That is it, at it's core - your ability, or inability to move the UTXO using your private key is EVERYTHING in Bitcoin.

What is important to understand about the Bitcoin blockchain is that it is unmoved and independent from most of the action and drama that surrounds the industry and the human trivialities. The blockchain simply carries on, day and night, producing blocks every 10 minutes.

The world's largest exchange got hacked and lost billions of dollars?
Bitcoin hit $1m per coin?
The Chinese government made Bitcoin illegal?

Doesn't matter, Bitcoin will just produce another block in the next 10 minutes, and another 10 minutes after that, as it has done every single day since it started. The next block will come, the difficulty of mining will adjust, the block reward will halve.

All of this will happen right on schedule, like it always has.

Like it always will.

5

Bitcoin Wallets

> *"Possession is 9/10 of the law"*
> — Thomas Draxe

In Bitcoin, the way in which people send and receive bitcoin among each other is through the use of what are known as 'bitcoin wallets'. In layman's terms, it's possible to simply imagine that the bitcoin you own sits inside the wallet, and you can send them to other people's wallets. All bitcoin that exists can be considered as sitting inside a wallet somewhere—the only exception is the bitcoin that has not yet been issued and is waiting to be given to miners; at which point, it will sit in their wallet.

As we covered in the previous chapter, bitcoins are represented by unspent transaction outputs (UTXOs), which are records of bitcoin amounts sent to your wallet that you have not yet spent.

So what is a Bitcoin wallet? Essentially, a Bitcoin wallet is just a pair of public and private keys, as we covered in Chapter Two. The two keys are just a long string of letters and numbers that do not mean anything to the human eye. The public key is used to derive the Bitcoin wallet address, and the private key is kept safe to sign transactions from this wallet.

Essentially, that is it—the receiving address and the key to be able to send any bitcoin that this address receives.

For example, I generated a new Bitcoin wallet right now to share the keys:

Public Key (Bitcoin wallet address):
1H19h2h6tx2a6xmkYMCPsdgdnf1Uz6FJDu

Private Key (To send bitcoin out from the wallet):
L4a2HW7rszpSx10xoijtSfVHmq9MvkmRJpzSqLV8bw2QW8osZLk4

Anyone could send bitcoin to that wallet address, and with the corresponding private key, one could send out any bitcoin received at that address. This works using the Public/Private Key pairing function we covered in Chapter Two. The important thing is to understand that a Bitcoin wallet needs to do two things:

1. Give a wallet address to receive bitcoin at.
2. Store the private key safely, so that you can spend the bitcoin later.

Generating a pair of keys is very easy, simply take a random number between 1 and 115,792,089,237,316,195,423,570,985,008,687,907,852,837,564,279,074,904,382,605,163,141,518,161,494,337. That is a number so incredibly large that it is hard to fathom, but effectively is almost as many possible bitcoin private keys as there are atoms in the known universe.

Each number in that range corresponds to a line of 64 characters and numbers in a unique arrangement, and that is then your Private key, like the one we gave as an example above.

The private key is used to generate a public key through elliptic curve multiplication, and the public key is then hashed to produce the wallet address. Bitcoin uses elliptic curve cryptography (ECC) for key generation, and it's not possible to derive the private key from the public key or wallet address. The result is a line of letters and numbers that is your public key—which is then hashed and encoded to produce your Bitcoin wallet address. You can receive bitcoin at this address, and when you want to send it, you use the private key to sign a message indicating you want to move it, specifying where to. Anyone can verify that the message you signed corresponds to the private key of that address without revealing the private key itself.

For the most part then, generating a pair of keys that form a wallet is very simple and quick to do. There are websites that allow you to create hundreds of wallets at a time and check if they have any bitcoin in them - they never do.

Equally, it would be possible to form valid Bitcoin wallet addresses without knowing the private key for them. One such example is:

1BitcoinEaterAddressDontSendf59kuE

This is a valid Bitcoin wallet address as it meets the requirements of the system, but it was not generated from a private key it was simply typed out to be comical. Any bitcoin sent to this wallet cannot be moved and is considered gone forever. It currently has almost 13 and a half bitcoin.

Another example is:

1CounterpartyXXXXXXXXXXXXXXXUWLpVr

This has over $57Million USD of bitcoin, lost forever.

Note that Bitcoin addresses cannot have a lowercase 'L' character in them, or an upper case 'i' as they looks too similar to each other or a '1'.

However, to be a valid address, the address has one final check to pass which is why:

1BitcoinTheU1timateGuidexxxzCMxj5

Is a valid address, but

1BitcoinTheU1timateGuidexxxxxxxxx

Is not.

This is because of what is known as a 'checksum', where the final 6 characters of the address are used to check the validity of the address. This is done by, essentially, taking the first part of the address and then running it through a hash algorithm and then taking the first 6 characters of that hashed output, then adding them to the end of the address.

For example, we take:

1BitcoinTheU1timateGuidexxx

And run it through a hashing algorithm and the output might be:

zCMxj56sGlkj824Dnflx9sD

We then take the first 6 characters from this and add it to the main part of the address to get:

1BitcoinTheU1timateGuidexxxzCMxj5

When attempting to send bitcoin to this address, the Bitcoin network takes the first 28 characters and runs the same hashing algorithm on them and checks that the final 6 characters of the address match the first 6 characters of the hash result. If they do, then the address is valid, if not it isn't.

This is useful as it means that if you mistype a character in the address, you can't send your bitcoin to that address. The system has a built-in way to check if you made a human error in the input and stop you from being able to send your bitcoin away forever. The checksum process means that the chance of accidentally typing an incorrect address is less than 1 in 4 million.

Generating a valid Bitcoin address, either with or without the private key is then very easy and simple to do. With a modern computer it takes less than a second to run the process and generate a pair of public and private keys that form a valid bitcoin wallet, which leads to the final little trick that we can do - vanity wallets.

Given the ease and speed of generating valid wallets, it's possible to run software to create many thousands of them over a short period of time and then search them for one that you like the look of. Historically, people have done this to generate what are known as 'vanity wallets'—much like vanity licence plates on cars.

By generating and exporting the keys for several thousand wallets, I was able to pick out two wallets that start with:

1DAN

Which are:
1DANQ9W9GjTTQsyHn6FRxeoENnLQFpdwML
1DAN6sT8iH5TVRiECK1h46P8eiaPd8Y7nN

Since the way we got to these was by generating the private and public keys, rather than just writing an arbitrary address and adding the checksum, these are addresses I own the private keys for and can spend any bitcoin received at them.

The main function of any Bitcoin wallet then comes primarily in protecting the private key from being exposed. As we will see in the various examples below, there are multiple ways to achieve this but the core principle is *always* the same and comes down to three fundamental points.

1. Never, ever, let your private key become known.
2. Anyone that knows your private key, effectively *owns* your bitcoin and can immediately deprive you of access to them.
3. If you do not own the private key, you do not own the bitcoin (Not Your Keys, Not Your Coin).

Exchange Wallets

These days, most people acquire bitcoin via exchanges, so that is a good place to start when explaining the various types of Bitcoin wallets that exist. Whilst buying bitcoin on exchanges is the most common method for most people to obtain bitcoin, it is also the method of holding bitcoin that causes the most anger from members of the Bitcoin community. There are a lot of things to consider when we contemplate how and where to hold onto our bitcoin.

If you open an account at a large exchange like Coinbase and purchase bitcoin there using your hard-earned money, the bitcoin will show in your account, and you have the ability to send it to anyone you want by inputting the destination wallet address. For most people, this is what they want and this fulfils all of their requirements. The sad reality is, for many people, understanding Bitcoin well enough to be able to competently hold their own private keys and not lose them or get hacked for them is simply something they have no time or desire to do.

The good thing about leaving bitcoin on an exchange is that you never have to worry about your phone getting hacked, you losing your private keys, or anything else—even if you forget your exchange password, you can just have it reset, and your bitcoin will be right there waiting for you. Also it's right there on the exchange for you to sell it for money any time you want, which adds another layer of convenience for the casual bitcoin investor. For a long time, as a bitcoin holder I personally held millions of dollars worth of bitcoin on various exchanges and would recommend that for most people it was the better option. But let's look into the downsides that come with leaving your bitcoin on exchanges.

Firstly, and this is the main one from which all the other problems come, you do not hold the private key for any of the bitcoin you have on an exchange account. Technically speaking, you don't own any bitcoin, you have an agreement with some company, somewhere, that you own some of the bitcoin that they hold the private keys to. The history of Bitcoin so far has shown that these agreements are often worthless and you may end up with nothing.

If the exchange loses the private keys, your bitcoin is gone.
If the exchange exposes the private keys, your bitcoin is gone.
If the exchange simply decides to keep your bitcoin, your bitcoin is gone.

There are many such cases, as we will cover in more detail later in the book, of exchanges getting hacked or even straight up fraud.

I personally still had around 1 bitcoin in FTX when it collapsed in November 2022. I held bitcoin on one of the biggest exchanges in the world, right up until the moment they collapsed and my bitcoin that I had there was gone. Thankfully, it was only around one bitcoin; at times in 2022, I held several million dollars' worth of bitcoin there.

For the most part, most exchanges are safe places to store your bitcoin and it is undoubtedly where most people start their journey, but you have to understand the trade off that is being made here between convenience and risk.

From a technical perspective, the exchange simply generates a new wallet address for you when you open an account there and stores the private key safely. Any bitcoin you send to that address, the exchange makes a note of and credits your account internally with that number of bitcoin, then moves your deposited coin into some big wallet that they control.
When you want to take your bitcoin off the exchange or send it to someone, the exchange simply uses its wallet of coins and sends checks if you have sufficient balance in your account before sending coins to the target wallet address you input. This typically uses a combination of what is often referred to as 'hot' and 'cold' wallets.

Hot Wallets & Cold Storage

All wallets are still essentially just a private key used to sign a transaction and move the bitcoin in the wallet associated with it, but the various methods of both keeping that key safe, and using it, have given birth to the idea of hot and cold wallets. It is common practice at large exchanges to have both hot and cold wallets for Bitcoin and other assets, as a form of security. Hot wallets, effectively, are simply any wallet that is connected to the internet and stores the private key in a way that is immediately accessible. Moreover in the case of exchanges it is a wallet that is capable of having transactions signed automatically without human oversight. Exchanges typically keep a small amount of Bitcoin in a hot wallet in order to facilitate people making withdrawals of Bitcoin from the exchange - these transactions happen all the time and use the systems the exchange has built, using wallets that are connected to the internet and can automatically sign transactions with the private key for them. This is obviously convenient, but with it again comes a compromise. Hot wallets are inherently more dangerous than cold wallets, as they can potentially be hacked or manipulated to send coins immediately.

Cold wallets, otherwise known as 'cold storage' are simply then methods of storing your private key in places or devices that are not connected to the internet and cannot be compelled to immediately sign transactions using the key. A very simple example of a cold storage wallet would be if you purchased a new laptop, never connected it to the internet, ran some bitcoin wallet generation software from a USB stick on the device, and generated your private key. If you then wrote your key down on a piece of paper and burned the laptop then ground its ashes into powder - an extreme example - you would be left with a Bitcoin wallet and connected private key that had never been anywhere near the internet and cannot be obtained from the device you used to create it.

In this case you could receive bitcoin to that wallet, but you would need to find some way in the future to use your private key to sign a transaction when you wanted to move the coins to another wallet.

Keeping your key offline and not immediately accessible helps to prevent hackers from stealing your coins, but comes with additional layers of inconvenience. As we have seen many times there are many aspects of Bitcoin, and life, where you have to find a balance between two extremes.

Hardware Wallets

A very popular way to hold your bitcoin recently has been via the use of 'hardware wallets'. These are dedicated small pieces of computer hardware that are used to store your private key and sign transactions using it. Two of the more prominent brands in this space are Trezor which were founded in 2013, and Ledger in 2014. In essence, the hardware wallets are all broadly the same; they are small devices that can be connected to a computer either directly or via a cable and can then send and receive information to the computer that is connected to the internet.

Hardware wallets typically also come with a dedicated suite of software to run on your computer and give some functionality such as generating a new wallet, sending transactions, backing up a private key, restoring a private key, etc.
With hardware wallets the key generation is typically done on the hardware device itself and the key is stored only on the device in a specialised chip known as the Hardware Security Module. When

you want to move the bitcoin using the private key stored on a hardware wallet, the software on your computer will build the transaction and send that data directly to the hardware wallet to be signed using the private key. The hardware wallet signs the message and then sends back to the computer the signed message only. This is important as in this case the private key never leaves the hardware device and is never exposed to the internet or the computer that may itself be compromised. Modern hardware wallets have touchscreen interfaces to review the transaction you are signing before it is signed by your private key, to check if the message from your computer has been in any way changed or corrupted before it reached the hardware device.

For the vast majority of people hardware wallets would be more than sufficient to store their bitcoin safely whilst taking full personal ownership of the private keys, but their use can be somewhat technical for those less experienced or comfortable with Bitcoin. It is also worth remembering that when holding your own private keys, if you lose them or expose them, your bitcoin is gone forever. There is no customer support to help you, when you hold your own keys, you are really on your own.

A final note on hardware wallets would be to mention the problems that Ledger customers have faced in recent years, due to problems with the handling of Ledger customer data. In July 2020, hackers were able to access the internal customer database of Ledger and steal the email addresses, and in many cases the names, home addresses, and telephone numbers of up to one million Ledger customers. This data was then used by criminals to either send phishing emails and viruses to Ledger users, and in some cases to threaten them with violence at their home address if they didn't hand over their bitcoin. Sadly this highlights another example of putting trust in a third party, in this case to handle your personal details correctly.

If you intend to use a hardware wallet, always be sure to purchase them directly from the manufacturer and never use a second hand device. The reason being that a device other than direct from the manufacturer with its tamper-proof seals intact may have been compromised to give your private key to a hacker.

Multi-Sig Wallets

Multi-sig wallets are a good option for increasing the security of your bitcoin wallet by requiring multiple private keys to be used to make any transactions. The way this works is you first decide how many keys you will generate for the wallet—each one being unique, not copies of the same key—and then how many of those keys will be required to meet the threshold to send a transaction.

For example, a two-of-three multi-sig wallet would require any two of the three generated keys to be used in order to send a transaction.

There is no limit to the number of keys specifically, but there is a limit in terms of the data size in the code which would thereby set a limit. Any transaction sending data above 100,000 bytes is considered non-standard and not accepted.

Most commonly two-of-three or three-of-five systems are used, but exchanges which hold billions of dollars of Bitcoin may have much higher numbers.
This helps increase the security of your Bitcoin holdings as if any private key is exposed, whoever has it can't steal your bitcoin. Any attacker would need to compromise enough keys to meet the 'm' in the m-of-n system set up.

This is also useful as a theft deterrence system for individuals that hold a large amount of bitcoin. If you hold bitcoin for the long term and dont need access to them in a hurry, it's a good idea to store them in a multi-sig wallet and then place the various keys in different places. This prevents anyone perpetrating what is known as a 'five dollar wrench' attack.

Let's say for example you hold bitcoin and have a three-of-five multi-sig wallet, you may wish to store the keys in the following way:

1. Key on a hardware wallet in your house.
2. Key on a different brand hardware wallet in your office.
3. Key on a wallet app on your phone.
4. Key on a hardware wallet device in a bank vault.
5. Key on a hardware wallet stored in a different country/state.

At any one time you can only be in possession of two keys at most - your phone and any key that is at the location you are at. Which is not enough to execute a transaction.
If an attacker came and threatened to beat you around the head with a five dollar wrench unless you gave him your bitcoin - you literally are not able to.

To do so you will need to travel, with the attacker either into your office building (in public and with security), a bank vault (public & security), or an airport and board a plane (public & security).
By distributing the location of the private keys, it adds this level of physical security similar to the security achieved by having Bitcoin miners geographically distributed.

Equally, the multi-sig approach gives you good redundancy in the keys so that if you lose a private key - house burns down, lose your phone in a boating accident, etc. then the remaining keys are still able to move the bitcoin and establish a new multi-sig wallet. Losing the key to a single-key wallet would be a fatal issue that meant your bitcoin was gone forever.

The downside, of course, is that the multi-sig approach means it takes longer and is more difficult for you to make a valid transaction when you wish to make a transaction - again we run into the universal idea of pro vs con of your choice of decision.

One company that offer multi-sig wallets for the general public is Casa, they have a strong Bitcoin focused team with good pedigree and offer a Multi-sig wallet as a service for a monthly fee. As of time of publication, I recommend them.

Seed Phrases

Given that any wallet then is essentially just a private key - which is just a long string of letters and numbers - we could simply write that down on a piece of paper and keep it safe.

We could then restore the wallet into some wallet software by entering the private key and would have access to our bitcoin again.

We then simply need to either write down or remember the private key string of characters, but copying them down exactly will be necessary, and without a single mistake. This can be challenging for many people to exactly record - much less commit to memory - a jumbled chain of 52 letters and numbers which also must be correctly capitalised.

To improve on this, in 2013 Bitcoin integrated an update that was suggested in the Bitcoin Improvement Proposal (BIP) 39 that allowed the seed phrase to be broken down into pieces and each assigned to a word from a known list of 2,048 words. The correct combination of 12 or 24 of these words would correctly translate to the core of the private key and the private key could be regenerated from that.

This makes sense if you consider each of the 2,048 words can be given a number between 0000 and 2048 and then by connecting them in a set of 24 you can generate a number that is 96 characters long (24 x 4) of blocks of 4 numbers between 0000 and 2048.

This results in almost 30 nonillion combinations, which in numbers is:

29,992,108,714,131,511,886,049,226,572,353,910,344,669,765,
097,528,240,399,535,871,084,188,884,059,340,801

Even if we only take 12 words (which is most common), we produce an order of numbers that is one of almost 5.5 duodecillion combinations, which in numbers is:

5,476,505,155,126,900,077,850,207,277,180,543,590,401

Which is sufficient. Remember all we need to do essentially when generating a bitcoin private key is pick a number and then run it through a hashing algorithm, so we essentially only need to store a big number somewhere, and:

conduct airport bind found dove voyage extend initial sunny derive camera age

Is a lot easier for humans to write down, recall, and remember, than:

1,992,021,528,572,420,652,486,635,471,316,723,731,921

This gives rise to another kind of method of storing your private key, known as a 'brain wallet'. Simply committing to memory the sequence of 12 words, you can carry your private key - and therefore your bitcoin - around in your head and then restore it into some software when you wish to make a transaction.

I personally have a brain wallet by storing 12 words in my head, but it's also backed up in other places and contains only a very small amount of money (less than $100). However, it's important to note that relying solely on memory can be risky due to the possibility of forgetting or misremembering.

Whenever you generate a wallet of any kind, it is always a good practice to generate the 12 or 24 word seed phrase for the private key and then make an offline copy of it. For many people that simply means writing it down, but others go to the extent of either embossing or engraving the seed phrase into a sheet of steel. This means that even in the event of a fire, the seed phrase will be recoverable. For a completely offline and unseizable Bitcoin wallet, you could generate a wallet offline, stamp the seed phrase into a steel plate, and then bury it somewhere on your property. As long as you remember where the seed phrase is buried, you can dig it up and recover the wallet and access your bitcoin - but anyone else is extremely unlikely to be able to access the wallet given that its cryptographically secure and the key is physically buried 6 feet deep in your garden somewhere.

It is best practice to back up a copy of your seed phrase, even if you are using a hardware wallet, in case the hardware wallet gets lost or damaged, you can restore your wallet onto a new device or other software.

Again, your seed phrase generates your private key, so it is as good as your private key. Never share it with anyone and keep it safely stored.

6

Bitcoin Scaling Solutions

> *"It's turtles all the way down"*
> — Bertrand Russell

In the 2009 whitepaper, Satoshi Nakamoto outlines Bitcoin as a 'Peer-to-Peer Electronic Cash System,' which it is. However, critics are quick to point out that the limitations on the Bitcoin blockchain prevent it from reaching real global adoption. The 10-minute time between blocks and the 4 MB maximum limit of data per block stifle the number of transactions per second (TPS) that the network can handle. Currently, the best estimate for calculating the equivalent TPS for Bitcoin's blockchain puts it around seven to ten TPS, which falls far short of alternatives such as the Visa network, which claims to process at up to 65,000 TPS.

There is also the final settlement time issue. As we discussed in previous chapters, the block time of ten minutes is chosen as a good mix between speed and preventing potential chain conflicts and splits. However, in reality, most transactions are not considered firmly confirmed until they are several blocks deep. This means that, even at a 10-minute-per-block interval—and remember, blocks can also take much longer to mine—you are looking at about an hour or so until a transaction would be finally settled with enough assurance for both sides.

In its base-level state, then, Bitcoin is not suitable for day-to-day payments—the classic example of using Bitcoin to buy a cup of coffee is clearly impractical given the time and potential cost of the transaction if the network is congested. Does this mean that Bitcoin has failed in its primary objective, namely to be a 'Peer-to-Peer Electronic Cash System'? Some people think so; this was one of the core reasons behind the 2017 chain forks and the block size wars that we will cover in a later chapter.

Given that Bitcoin is legal tender in El Salvador, it is accepted in coffee shops and McDonald's. You can literally, today, walk into a McDonald's, buy coffee with Bitcoin, and walk out in minutes— much less time than the 10 minutes it would take to mine a single block on the chain. So how are they able to do this?

To scale Bitcoin, we need to move from the idea that it can be used only as the layer of final settlement and understand that day-to-day transactions between people can be moved off the Bitcoin chain. If you think about it, this is essentially what Visa does in the traditional payments space. If we think back to the example we outlined in Chapter Two of using a Visa card to pay for a coffee in Indonesia, the payments all happen on the Visa network, but no money actually changes hands until the end of the day when Visa reconciles all of the transactions and batches them into single transfers between banks.

Rather than banks having to make a final settlement between each other every time someone buys a coffee, transactions are bundled into the final total, and then a single transaction is made much later—in the case of Visa, once per day. In comparison, Bitcoin's circa 60-minute wait is much faster than Visa's once-a-day settlement, but nobody would suggest that Visa is impractical for day-to-day transactions, so where is the disconnect here?

Well, we need to understand that comparing Visa transactions to Bitcoin blockchain transactions is not a fair apples-to-apples comparison. We are comparing Visa's initial confirmations with Bitcoin's final settlement. Once something is paid with a Visa card, there is still time to reverse the transaction, because although it is cleared and your bank has said you're good for the money, the final settlement to the other party's bank has not been made.
Conversely, with Bitcoin on the main blockchain, there is *only* final confirmation. Broadly speaking, unless you are extremely unfortunate that the block your transaction gets into happens to be one where two miners conflict and both discover a block at the same time—and one miner didn't include your transaction in their block, and that miner subsequently forms the longest chain (something that is incredibly unlikely to ever happen)—then as soon as your transaction is included in a block, it is final, forever.

What we need to develop for Bitcoin is a system where transactions can happen quickly and get instant settlement but are given final settlement on the main Bitcoin chain only later and when necessary.

To give a real-world analogy, imagine two golfers are playing a round of golf and are competing with each other. They decide that after each hole, they will both return to the clubhouse and update their score in the master log book there. This is obviously troublesome and causes congestion in the clubhouse as everyone clamours to write in the main log book. Instead of doing this, the golfers decide to take a piece of paper and pen with them and record their scores after each hole. Then, once they return to the clubhouse, they simply update their final score in the log book. This is an example of taking reporting off the main record by maintaining a side record, which is then used to update the main record later.

That is essentially how all Layer 2 scaling solutions work in Bitcoin: by moving the recording of transactions off the Bitcoin chain and then updating the chain later when they finalise all of the transactions they wish to make.

There has been a lot of work in this area, and we can take a look at some of the leading ideas and how they work in practice.

Lightning Network

Perhaps the most well-known Bitcoin scaling solution is the Lightning Network, a Layer 2 solution launched in 2016. The Lightning Network is essentially a parallel network to the

Bitcoin blockchain and works by establishing networks of two-party channels that together form a massive network.

In the Lightning Network 2 parties open a channel by setting up a multi-sig wallet that requires both parties to sign off on a transaction. For example, if Alice and Bob decide to open a Lightning channel together, each puts 1 bitcoin into the multisig wallet. At the same time, they both sign a bitcoin transaction to send 1 bitcoin back to themselves each, but importantly, this transaction is not published to the Bitcoin chain.

This means that the lightning channel holds 2 bitcoin, 1 from each party, and either party can publish the signed transaction to the Bitcoin chain and get their bitcoin back.

Now, if Alice wants to send Bob 0.5 bitcoin via the Lightning Network channel, they do the following:

1. Alice signs a new transaction that pays 1.5 bitcoin to Bob and 0.5 bitcoin to herself.
2. Bob also signs the same transaction - so now it is able to be executed if either side wants to push it back onto the Bitcoin chain.
3. Both parties cancel their previous transaction that they signed that paid out 1 bitcoin each.

With that, we have effectively moved 0.5 bitcoin from Alice to Bob, without ever using the Bitcoin chain.

Alice or Bob could now decide to exit the lightning network and close the channel by publishing the unpublished signed transaction. This would send 1.5 of the bitcoin, from the 2 bitcoin wallet, to Bob and 0.5 bitcoin to Alice.

For as long as they want to continue using the lighting network, Alice and Bob can just continue to sign, but not publish, updated transactions and share them with each other, adjusting the balance each other owns. This can happen infinite times, without ever touching the Bitcoin chain until they decide to exit the network and get their bitcoin back by pushing the most recent signed transaction to the Bitcoin chain and dividing the bitcoin in the shared wallet according to the up to date balance.

This is fine for sending funds between Alice and Bob, but lightning network channels can only ever trade bitcoin back and forth amongst themselves, and nobody else. This is where the network element comes into play.

Let's imagine the same scenario as above, with Alice and Bob having an open channel on the Lightning Network with 1 bitcoin each. Additionally, Bob has a second channel open with Charlie, in which they also have 1 bitcoin each.

Alice has no direct channel to Charlie, but the Lightning Network makes it possible for her to route a payment via Bob to Charlie in the following way.

Imagine Alice wants to send 0.25 bitcoin to Charlie. The lightning network detects that there is a path between Alice and Charlie via Bob and sets up the following set of transactions:

Alice will send 0.25 bitcoin to Bob (by updating their signed but unpublished multi-sig transaction)

Bob will send 0.25 bitcoin to Charlie (the same way)

Now the two channels look like the following:

Channel between Alice and Bob:
Alice: 0.75 bitcoin
Bob: 1.25 bitcoin

Channel between Bob and Charlie:
Bob: 0.75 bitcoin
Charlie: 1.25 bitcoin

Bob gained 0.25 bitcoin on his channel with Alice but lost 0.25 on his channel with Charlie, which makes him net even.

Alice lost 0.25, and Charlie gained 0.25, which is the correct state to be expected in a transaction where Alice sends 0.25 bitcoin to Charlie.

It is possible to build a path via several points to go from the sender to the recipient, the network looks for the most efficient path and cheapest fees - as each point in the path may charge a small fee, typically a fraction of a penny.

Given that all that happens here is signing but not publishing new transactions, the lightning network can route payments across the network in fractions of a second. Once the recipient and amount is known, the network already finds the right path and gets ready to update all of the unpublished transactions and once the sender hits the send button the network just instantly updates.

All of this means that actual bitcoin can move between people, irrevocably, in seconds and in most cases for next to zero cost. This makes it ideal for small amounts and is the primary method by which bitcoin is used in day-to-day low-value transactions. The TPS for the Lightning Network is reported to be up to 1 million, which would make it more than capable for global adoption.

Lightning network is used extensively in El Salvador and is the main way in which bitcoin is exchanged between people and merchants. It is accepted in leading stores such as McDonalds and Starbucks and is integrated in the state issued mobile wallet application.

Given that the transactions on lightning are all peer-to-peer and updating but not publishing transactions to the Bitcoin chain, all transactions on the lightning network are non-public and there is no way to track them. This is the opposite to Bitcoin main chain where all transactions are public. For this reason, lightning offers some additional privacy, but also makes it impossible to know how widespread adoption of the technology is.

The main advantages of the lightning network are that it transacts using real bitcoin and you always retain possession of your bitcoin at all times – it does not have any trusted third party. Also the network is decentralised and distributed, much like Bitcoin, and has no central point of failure. Both of which make the lightning network very much in line with the ethos of Bitcoin.

The disadvantages of the lightning network are few but worth mentioning. Firstly, the technology is much newer and does not have the strong track record that Bitcoin has been able to develop over time. Secondly, the network is less robust to attack than the Bitcoin main chain. Finally, the capacity of any transaction is limited by the size of the Lightning Network channels. It would not be possible to send 20 bitcoin easily across the network as most channels are below 0.5 bitcoin in size which mens they cannot facilitate transactions bigger than that, and also the channels need to be periodically rebalanced otherwise they become only able to receive or send but not both. In the above examples, Bob can now only send 0.75 to Charlie as his sending capacity is reduced due to sending 0.25 on Alice's behalf. Charlie could route 0.25 bitcoins via Bob in order to rebalance the channel and restore Bob's full capacity to send 1 bitcoin. This periodical rebalancing can be automated but is an issue that limits the liquidity and capacity of the network.

Wrapped Bitcoin

Another method for transacting bitcoin outside of the main Bitcoin chain is to use another blockchain as the means of transaction. This is a popular and common way to transact with Bitcoin and to allow Bitcoin to be used in other chains, financial products, and protocols. These chains can also act as a Layer 2 scaling solution, allowing you to move Bitcoin between people without using the main Bitcoin chain. This is achieved by having a trusted party that takes in Bitcoin on the main Bitcoin chain and then issues tokens on the new chain, which represent the Bitcoin they have in storage.

For example, WBTC is a wrapped bitcoin token that exists on the Ethereum chain. You can either buy the WBTC directly on exchanges or can send bitcoin to the company behind the issuance of the token and have your native chain bitcoin exchanged with tokenised WBTC on the Ethereum chain. If you wish to redeem your WBTC for native bitcoin, you can simply send your WBTC to the company and get your native bitcoin back. The wrapped bitcoin then basically acts as a receipt for one's original bitcoin, much in the same way that original paper money was just a receipt for gold stored at the goldsmith's.

There are wrapped bitcoin on many chains, including Ethereum, Solana, Polygon, and others. These offer many benefits such as increased speed of transaction, higher TPS, one confirmation finality, etc. Some of these chains also allow users to use bitcoin in decentralized financial systems, such as posting Bitcoin as collateral for a loan.

The main downside with these tokenised or wrapped bitcoin is that they always involve a trusted third party and require users to give up ownership of their original bitcoin. If the company holding the bitcoin gets hacked, the bitcoin can be stolen and then the tokens are worthless. Equally, the company could issue a load of tokens that are not actually backed by bitcoin, or the smart contract could be hacked to issue additional tokens, which would drastically devalue users' tokenised bitcoin. Finally, tokenised or wrapped bitcoin also requires users to place trust in the chain that it is issued on to continue to operate. Solana for example is a chain that often goes offline for periods of time, during which the tokenised bitcoin can't be moved. Also, if the chain gets called into question for any reason, the price of the token can meaningfully de-peg from the price of bitcoin—as happened with the Solana wrapped bitcoin during the collapse of the cryptocurrency exchange FTX.

Whilst tokenised/wrapped bitcoin has a purpose and can alleviate congestion on the main Bitcoin chain, there are some significant risks associated with it. Unless you need to use your bitcoin in a way that interacts with financial tools on those specific chains, there is no benefit to holding your bitcoin in a tokenised form on another chain. This introduces a new counterparty risk.

Exchanges

Another way to send and receive bitcoin without using the main Bitcoin chain is via centralised cryptocurrency exchanges. As we will cover in later chapters, centralised cryptocurrency exchanges are places to buy and sell bitcoin and work by taking ownership of your bitcoin and crediting your internal account balance on their platform.
Many exchanges also allow for free and instant internal transfers of bitcoin between users. This can be considered as a layer 2 type solution as it facilitates transferring of bitcoin without using the main Bitcoin chain.

This is possible because the exchange holds all of the bitcoin and can simply make an adjustment to their internal database. I often use Crypto.com to send bitcoin to my friend in Thailand, simply because I have some bitcoin on there already and I know he has a Crypto.com account. If I have 1 Bitcoin in my Crypto.com account and I send 0.1 bitcoin to my friend, Crypto.com simply updates our balances on their platform, and no bitcoin ever moves on-chain. My balance is updated to 0.9 and Jon's balance gets an additional 0.1 bitcoin. This means the most I can withdraw is now 0.9 bitcoin and not the 1 bitcoin I had before.

Sending bitcoin to other users within a cryptocurrency exchange is probably the fastest and cheapest (free) way of moving bitcoin, but again it comes with a list of downsides. Firstly, it requires you to hold your bitcoin on an exchange where you do not hold the private keys. This is problematic if the exchange collapses—as FTX did—as you then lose any bitcoin that you held there. I personally held some bitcoin on FTX when it collapsed. It's now gone forever.

As we mentioned in earlier chapters, unless you hold the private key to the bitcoin, you don't actually own the bitcoin. I would say that the ability to use a centralised exchange as a means to send bitcoin to others is more a side effect of the utility of centralised exchanges and certainly not the main focus. That said, if you have some bitcoin left on an exchange it is easier and quicker to do an internal transfer to another user rather than process an on chain transaction; but in general it's a bad idea to leave bitcoin on centralised exchanges in any meaningful amount.

Physical Transfers

Another potential way to exchange bitcoin without using the Bitcoin network is via physical transfer of the private keys. As established in previous chapters, possession of the private keys to bitcoin equates to ownership of the bitcoin. If someone else has your private key, they effectively have your bitcoin. Theoretically, then, it is possible to transfer ownership of bitcoin simply by giving the private keys to another party. If I hold 10 bitcoin in a wallet and I write down the seed phrase for that wallet on a piece of paper, I can simply pass that piece of paper to the next person and effectively transfer the bitcoin to them.

The main problem with this, however (as some of you may have already realised), is that the recipient of the seed phrase cannot be sure that I have not made a copy of it, either in my head or in writing—and thus could also move the Bitcoin after I have given them the key.

There are some creative technological ways around this. One method that I have used is with specially designed USB hardware wallets called OPENDIME. The device plugs into a USB port of a computer and generates a new Bitcoin wallet with a public key and a private key. The private key is stored in a special module on the USB stick. In order to access the private key, you have to poke a pin through the device to break a circuitry connection, at which point the private key is accessible and the funds on the wallet can be sent.

If the private key has not yet been accessed, the USB flashes a green LED light, which shows to anyone that the private key is not known to anyone. The device will show the balance held on the wallet and can sign a message using the private key to verify that the USB device contains the key for the wallet. Once the device has been poked with a pin, the LED flashes red, and the device shows on the computer that the key is compromised and known.

Provided you trust the hardware and the software of the device, this is a theoretical way of moving bitcoin without touching the Bitcoin chain by performing physical transfer of private keys in a trusted way. However it doesn’t scale at all and is perhaps better used as a way to obtain bitcoin anonymously rather than anything else.

7

Bitcoin Updates & Forks

> *"If nothing ever changed, there would be no butterflies"*
> — Maya Angelou

Over the 15 years since Bitcoin was first introduced, the system has gone through many changes, but as Satoshi himself outlined, the majority of the code remains essentially the same as it was in the whitepaper. Given that there is no central body that can just push out updates to the code, the process for updating Bitcoin is often a long and drawn out process requiring the buy-in of many decentralised parties in order to reach consensus.

Anyone can submit an idea to update Bitcoin by using the process known as the Bitcoin Improvement Proposal system to submit a 'BIP' that is given a sequential number (BIP1, BIP2, etc.) which then gets reviewed by the broader community before it is potentially integrated by people into their own versions of the software that they run. Any proposed update is also rigorously tested on the Bitcoin Testnet before it is rolled out to the main network.

Bitcoin Testnet

The Bitcoin testnet is essentially a parallel version of the Bitcoin network that runs the same software as the main network but holds no meaningful value in financial terms. This system is run by volunteers that run nodes and mine blocks, but because of the lack of financial incentive in the network, it has far fewer participants and miners, which also makes it less secure than the main network. Any new changes that are proposed to the Bitcoin network are first deployed onto this testing network so that it can be checked and proven before it is allowed to be rolled out on the main Bitcoin chain. This is typical of any modern software update process outside of Bitcoin, with all major software companies testing their changes on a smaller, often private, version of their software before putting it live into their main system. The advantage that other software systems have, however, is that any updates that later turn out to be bad, or troublesome, can quickly reverse the changes with little harm. For example, if Facebook rolls out a new update that inadvertently allows people outside their friends list to see their status updates, that might cause some problems. Facebook might get in trouble, lose reputation, or pay a fine if it is egregious, but it would be quickly reversed and the problem solved. The distributed and self-ownership nature of Bitcoin, plus the fact that all transactions are final and irreversible make this effectively impossible on Bitcoin. If an update to Bitcoin made it possible for someone to steal billions of dollars of bitcoin, which they could then cash out immediately to Swiss, Russian, or Cayman Island bank accounts, then that would potentially prove to be a fatal issue for the entire Bitcoin project, inflicting hundreds of billions of dollars of economic damage on innocent people. For this reason, Bitcoin is like a large supermassive cargo ship travelling the ocean, for which any changes in course are slow and methodical, rather than a fast and nimble speedboat that can turn on a dime.

The Bitcoin testnet, then, is a vital part of the overall Bitcoin network but, importantly, is entirely segregated from the main Bitcoin chain. There is no way to move bitcoin from the testnet over to the main Bitcoin chain and vice versa. Proposed changes and updates can fail on the testnet without any impact on the main Bitcoin network.

Blocksize Wars

The most contentious of updates so far came in 2017, in a period that is often referred to as the 'Blocksize Wars', during which the Bitcoin community saw disagreements and splits over proposed updates to the Bitcoin network regarding how much data should be included in each block. As we covered in previous chapters, the maximum size of a Bitcoin block is nominally 1 megabyte, given that this is what the community feels is a good balance between transactional capacity and the speed at which the network grows in size. In an effort to increase the number of transactions the Bitcoin network can process, there were parts of the Bitcoin community that sought to increase the maximum size of Bitcoin blocks, potentially as high as 20MB per block, in order to fit more transactions into each block and increase the capacity of the Bitcoin network. Proposals put forward to enact this upgrade caused division in the community, with strong opinions held on both sides, and at times there seemed to be no clear path forward as to what the ultimate outcome would be. This is where the inherent decentralised nature of Bitcoin was shown in full effect as the system that it is, one in which each party acts independently and in what they view to be their best interests. A subset of the Bitcoin community decided that they would implement these changes to increase the size of blocks on the blockchain. This update would not be compatible with any other members of the network that refused to implement their update, in a process known as a 'hard fork'.

Hard forks occur when a change is made by some members of the system that is not compatible with those that don't, and effectively splits the blockchain into two separate chains. This was not the first hard fork of Bitcoin; there have been many before and will likely be many afterwards. In fact, anyone can hard fork the Bitcoin chain at any time. I could write an update to the Bitcoin software that says I get ownership of the over 1 million bitcoins that Satoshi owns and then decide to run that software on my own version of Bitcoin. This would create a hard fork, and nobody else would have any interest in it, and I would be left with a fork of Bitcoin that nobody acknowledges, in which I own a lot of 'bitcoin' that are utterly worthless, much as if I took a piece of paper and wrote £1,000,000 on it; nobody would accept that as a valid banknote. Any fork of the Bitcoin network is only valid if it has a large community buy-in at a human level—because Bitcoin is not just a technological protocol; it relies on human consensus assigning value to it. This is the same reason that the Bitcoin testnet bitcoins hold no value despite the technology being almost identical to the main Bitcoin network.

Bitcoin Cash

And so it came to be in August 2017 that a subset of the Bitcoin community pushed forward with their plan to fork the Bitcoin chain and create a hard fork with an 8MB block size limit, creating the first meaningful hard fork that did not enjoy the support of the vast majority of the Bitcoin community. This new chain was called Bitcoin Cash and was led by prominent Bitcoin enthusiast Roger Ver with a vision to create a Bitcoin network that had substantially more transaction capacity to facilitate many times more transactions per second at a much lower cost than the original Bitcoin chain. Given that this was a fork of the original chain, anyone that held bitcoin before the fork was given the same number of bitcoin on the Bitcoin Cash fork and could move them simply by using their existing wallet and private keys on this new forked network.

Despite the technologically increased transaction capacity, Bitcoin Cash has since failed to find meaningful market adoption. The price of each Bitcoin Cash hit a peak in USD terms of around $3,800 per coin on 2nd August, the day after its launch, and is down some 97% since then. When denominated in Bitcoin terms, Bitcoin Cash has fallen over 98% since its peak.

This, again, shows that Bitcoin's power lies not simply in its technology but in the adoption and acceptance of this by people in aggregate. A fundamental understanding, anything only has value insofar as people are willing to pay you for it.

There is no method by which Bitcoin Cash could integrate back into the main Bitcoin chain now, as there are millions of transactions that occurred on that chain that did not occur on the main Bitcoin chain, making it impossible to reconcile the two.

Bitcoin Cash is not Bitcoin.

Bitcoin Satoshi Vision

Following the hard fork of Bitcoin Cash in August 2017, the group that created this hard fork still had further internal fighting about the best path forward for their vision of Bitcoin. This internal fighting ultimately culminated in November of 2018 in a farcical case of 'People Front of Judea' in which a faction of this new Bitcoin Cash group decided they too would like to take their ball and go home, and create their own hard fork of the Bitcoin Cash chain.

Led by the leading Satoshi Nakamoto tribute act that is Craig Wright, a group of the Bitcoin Cash community executed a fork of the Bitcoin Cash chain in November of 2018 to create a new version of Bitcoin that they named 'Bitcoin Satoshi Vision' in which the blocksize was substantially increased, and the chain also granted Craig Wright full access to all of the bitcoin held by the original Satoshi wallets (over 1 million bitcoin).

Once again, this fork failed to gain any meaningful adoption and despite being supported by many exchanges, it was ultimately removed from most places people can buy cryptocurrency - due in no small part to the legal troubles and litigious nature of Wright.

Bitcoin Satoshi Vision has fallen over 98% against Bitcoin since its inception.

Bitcoin Satoshi Vision is not Bitcoin.

Segwit

A less contentious solution to the scaling problems of Bitcoin was also put forward in 2017 that would be backwards compatible and would not cause a hard fork of the network. This update is known as the Segregated Witness update or 'SegWit' for short. The SegWit update was a change to the code of the Bitcoin network that would keep the core block size at 1MB but also allow an expanded total block size of 4MB in an expanded section of a block. This allowed the core block size to remain 1MB in size - and thus backwards compatible - whilst also allowing the expanded block to include a lot more data and thus transactions. Essentially this update works in the following way:
Traditionally, all of the data of a transaction is included in the 1MB Bitcoin block which contains all of the signatures from the private keys and all other verifying data. This is required so that anyone auditing the chain can see all of the signatures and data and verify that the transactions are valid - however this data takes up a lot of space in the block and uses space that could be freed up for other transactions.

This is where the SegWit upgrade comes in; the change introduces the concept of 'block weight,' allowing for a maximum block weight of 4 million units without increasing the base block size limit of 1MB. This effectively increases the capacity of each block without altering the fundamental block size, maintaining backward compatibility. The witness data, which can be up to an additional 3MB, is not recognised by nodes that have not upgraded to SegWit, but the 1MB base block remains compatible, allowing non-upgraded nodes and miners to continue functioning without interruption. This gives the upgrade its backwards compatibility with nodes and miners that choose not to update.

To achieve this, the bitcoin UTXOs that are sent to SegWit upgraded wallets are essentially converted to be UTXOs (bitcoin) that can be spent without a signature, so that they can be spent inside a regular 1MB block without any accompanying signature.

However, the signature data is sent in the extended block which is seen and read by SegWit upgraded nodes and miners. This means that the non-upgraded nodes would see the transactions as valid, and the SegWit upgraded nodes would verify the signature in the extended block and deny the transactions if the signature in the extended block was not correct. This effectively pushes the security of those transactions to the SegWit upgraded nodes to verify and to prevent bad actors attempting to spend these new UTXOs without the valid signatures.

Given that the network relies on consensus, this remains safe provided there are sufficient SegWit nodes and miners on the network to reject any invalid SegWit transactions.

Importantly, for this to work best, the network would need to have Bitcoin miners upgrade to the SegWit update and have them prevent invalid SegWit transactions from entering the blocks that they mine - this once again leads to a very interesting application of economic game theory in the Bitcoin network in that miners cannot afford to include an invalid transaction in their blocks and risk them being rejected by the network, as to do so would mean their work on finding the block would be wasted and they get no financial reward for the electricity they spent to mine it. However, this incentive to adopt SegWit was not taken up as readily as would normally be expected by the large Bitcoin mining organisations; it would later transpire that this was because the update would close a secret loophole that some large miners were using to increase their ability to mine Bitcoin, and so they had a personal financial incentive to prevent the update from rolling out.

This, along with the fact that the SegWit update was being pushed out during the very contentious blocksize wars, lead to some strong disagreement on if or how to roll out the SegWit update, and ultimately lead to the first ever 'User Activated Soft Fork' (UASF).

In addition, the SegWit update also fixed a few known issues with something known as 'transaction malleability' whereby a part of the transaction could be slightly changed without invalidating the signature that was used to send it. For example if a transaction contained a '1' this could be changed to be a '01' or '001' and the signature would remain valid. This could change the function of the transaction and meant in some cases it could be modified before it was fully locked into the network.

UASF

The SegWit update was broadly favoured by nodes and users of Bitcoin, but faced some resistance from Bitcoin miners. This created a disagreement between the two largest stakeholders in the network. As the participants that expend billions of dollars and energy annually to mine new blocks, miners hold a lot of power in the Bitcoin network and many felt they could not be compelled to update to SegWit if they didn't want to.

Conversely, running a Bitcoin node can be done easily on a $100 laptop and costs only a few dollars a year in electricity to run, but provides a core and vital service of maintaining a geographically, politically diverse check on the entire network that validates all transactions.

Both are required to maintain the Bitcoin network.

As with all updates, miners are given a ramp up time to signal if they agree or disagree with change and if they have implemented the required update. This is done via toggling an arbitrary byte of data in the blocks they produce to be either a 1 or a 0, which shows if they have updated yet or not.
As the summer of 2017 drew on and miners had not adopted the SegWit upgrade at the rate that users were hoping for. Some proposed an alternate update known as SegWit2x, which would implement the update as long as the block size also increased to 2MB from the existing 1MB. Many people still opposed any blocksize increase and a community grew around the idea of a new update to the Bitcoin network that would effectively force miners to update, this was BIP148 and employed financial game

theory to coerce the miners to update.
The update effectively was that nodes would update and would reject any new mined block that had not yet updated to the SegWit upgrade.
This is a very interesting play, as the miners absolutely need the nodes to validate their blocks, or they can be rejected from the network and the vast amount of money and energy spent on mining the block would be wasted. The risk of having a newly found block be rejected by the nodes, and therefore by the network, is a significant financial risk to any miner. Given that the majority of nodes on the bitcoin network were in favour of the upgrade, and those against it had - or could - fork off onto the Bitcoin Cash chain, this update was accepted by the nodes and brought this financial risk to the Bitcoin miners - essentially to update to SegWit or risk their new blocks being invalid and receiving no reward for the work they did in finding blocks.

Typically, all updates to the Bitcoin network were essentially 'miner activated' whereby the updates had to be adopted by 95% of miners before they were deployed onto the network.
In this novel 'User Activated' update the nodes put forward a path where this limit need not be reached for them to implement the changes and force miners to make a decision to join them or exit the network. This broke the previous model which would allow just 5% of the mining power to veto an update and made plain a new understanding.

Miners are not paid to dictate the rules of the Bitcoin network, they are paid to follow the rules of the network.

The UASF was successful and in the weeks up to the implementation date of SegWit the majority of miners upgraded to the SegWit update. In doing so, the alternate proposal of increasing the blocksize to 2MB was also discarded and the original implementation of SegWit went live on the network on the 1st August 2017.

Some miners chose to continue mining only on the Bitcoin Cash fork, but the majority of the network remained and Bitcoin continued to grow from strength to strength with the SegWit update fully locked in.

The UASF was an important time in the history of Bitcoin and pivotal in showing that no one group has control over its direction and future.

Taproot

The most significant update to Bitcoin since SegWit came on the 14th November 2021 with the implementation of BIPs 340, 341 & 342, more commonly known collectively as 'Taproot'.

The Taproot update added significant new functionality to the Bitcoin network with regard to how transactions can be processed, and increasing the privacy that can be afforded to users making those transactions.

Firstly, the update allows an upgrade to the method in which signatures for transactions are encoded, moving from the traditional method of Elliptic Curve Digital Signature Algorithm (ECDSA) signatures to a more secure, modern method known as

Schnorr Signatures. This is essentially just a technical update in the method used to generate a signature from a private key and is an extremely technical and cryptographic issue—but essentially it's just a new method that is more secure, quicker, and takes up less space to process. Without getting into the weeds on the technicalities of this change, a main benefit is that multiple signatures can now be combined into a single hashed output. For example, a multi-sig wallet that requires 10 signatures to spend the UTXO would previously require all 10 signatures to be sent with the transaction, taking up 10 times the block space of a single signature—the new upgrade allows all 10 signatures to be hashed into a single signature output, taking up only one-tenth of the space. Additionally, the inputs that are being combined do not need to be revealed to the Bitcoin chain and as a result the inputs are hidden from the public.
This means that a transaction requiring 3 of 5 signatures would be able to be processed without anyone knowing which of the 3 of the 5 parties had signed. It also means that the output transaction would not even reveal that it was a multi-sig transaction at all, as the output would contain the same single signature as any other transaction. This has the benefit of improving the privacy of those making the transaction and reducing blocksize use - which in turn means that more transactions can be processed per block, increasing the TPS of the network.

Whilst these updates are important for privacy, security, and scalability, the main impact of the Taproot update came in the final part of the proposed upgrade, the Tapscript upgrade.

The Tapscript update essentially expanded on the existing code that can be used within the Bitcoin network and expanded the available operation codes or 'OP codes' that are used within the software to handle and process transactions. This new form of scripting in the Tapscript update made much more complex conditional transactions both viable and possible to execute with enhanced privacy. For example, using the new Tapscript update, it would be possible to make a bitcoin transaction predicated on a series of potential triggers to validate the transaction. Whilst typically a transaction would simply be predicated on a valid signature from the UTXO owner, the combined Tapscript and Schnorr signatures now mean that multiple possible conditions can be combined into a single signature and any one of them being met can produce the valid signature to authorise the transfer.

For example, a wallet containing 10 bitcoin could be scripted to have 4 possible triggers that would produce a valid signature to move the bitcoin.

1. If Alice signs using her private key
2. If Bob and Charlie both sign using their keys
3. If the date is after 31st December 2024
4. If some specific data criteria is met

By using the Tapscript and Schnorr Signatures, the outcome of each of those four paths can be hashed to produce a string that represents the conditions being met, but since it is a hash, there is no way of working backwards from it to understand what its input is.

Let's say in our example that Alice signs using her private key. This is enough to generate a valid signature to move the bitcoin in the wallet, but how does this work?

Alice signs the transaction and generates an output using her signature, she then takes this and combines it with the hashed outputs of the other 3 conditions, which when combined together through the Schnorr signature process generates a valid signature to move the bitcoin. This data is passed to the blockchain via the miners, who validate it as a correct and authorised transaction. But since they only see the hashed outputs of the other three conditions, nobody can know what those conditions were. Only the use of Alice's private key to generate the signature is passed as data to the blockchain to be stored in the witness data of the block.

This validation data from Alice's signature is stored in the witness data of the transaction and associated with this transaction. But the use of Tapscript means that this validation data need not have been a signature; it could have been any other condition that was met and could be any arbitrary data. This unintentionally became one of the major developments that came from the Taproot upgrade.

Overall, the Taproot upgrade added more complex functionality to Bitcoin and increased the level of security of the network. The upgrade was far less contentious than SegWit but will probably best be remembered more for the unforeseen and unintended consequences of the update, which led to the birth of the ability to store arbitrary data natively on the Bitcoin blockchain—leading to the rise of Bitcoin 'NFTs' and tokens through the use of 'ordinals' and 'inscriptions'.

Ordinals & BRC20 tokens

The Taproot update rolled out into the Bitcoin network in November 2021, and little much changed in the immediate period. This was until January 2023 when a software engineer named Casey Rodarmor figured out a method of using the Taproot update as a means for storing arbitrary data on the network, and then essentially binding or 'inscribing' that data to a single satoshi (0.00000001 of a bitcoin) thereby creating what are essentially 'non-fungible tokens' on the Bitcoin chain.

To take a step back, let's first cover what non-fungible tokens are. If you're reading this, then by now you will most likely have heard of 'NFTs' which were a cryptocurrency related mania that swept through the public consciousness over the last 4-5 years with people trading jpegs of monkeys for millions of dollars. To understand this, we first need to understand what 'fungible' and 'non-fungible' mean. Essentially 'fungible' means that any one item is the same as another item - a gram of gold is the same as any other gram of gold, a $1 bill is the same as any other $1 bill, etc. These are all fungible. An oil painting is not the same as any other oil painting - for example a Picasso is not the same as an oil painting from your local car-boot sale. This, essentially, is the difference and why non-fungible tokens have a distinct value - they are tokens that are one of a kind and not comparable with other tokens.

In Ethereum, this is done by generating unique tokens as new tokens on top of the Ethereum chain, and this is how most networks handle NFTs.

In Bitcoin, with ordinals, the approach is different in that we take an existing part of the Bitcoin network - a single satoshi - and then attach arbitrary data to that token itself. This is perhaps why the nomenclature here is different; rather than 'minting' an NFT as you would on Ethereum or other chains, in Ordinals the 'NFT' is 'inscribed' much like one might inscribe a message on the side of a silver coin.

So how do we leverage the Taproot update to bind arbitrary data to specific satoshis?

First of all let's look at where the name 'ordinals' comes from, this is a mathematical term 'ordinal numbers' that essentially just means consequential numbers used for counting something, e.g. 'one, two, three, etc.' This numbering process is used to number every single satoshi since the genesis block back in 2009, so the first ever block mined generated 50 bitcoin, which is 50 x 100 million satoshis so that block contains satoshis numbered 1 - 5,000,000,000. The next block generated the satoshis numbered 5,000,000,001 - 10,000,000,000 etc. In doing so we create non-fungibility among the individual satoshis as each now has a unique number and satoshi number 10 is not the same as satoshi number 5, for example.

Now, to bind these satoshis with arbitrary data, we simply use the newfound abilities in the Taproot update in the following way:

1. Create a Taproot enabled bitcoin wallet
2. Deposit some bitcoin there
3. Create a condition to generate a valid signature to send the bitcoin

4. Fulfill that condition, have the condition data written to the chain and move 1 satoshi to a target wallet

In doing so, the single satoshi is moved to the target wallet, and the condition that was met to generate the valid signature is committed to the Bitcoin blockchain in the witness data of the block. Now, that satoshi is connected to that arbitrary data that was used to generate the signature to send it.
Given that the Tapscript update means that the data in the validation condition can be, essentially, anything, all we have to do is post the data we wish to bind or 'inscribe' to the satoshi as the condition to be met: i.e 'if I submit this data to you, check it is the same as the condition data, then approve the transaction'.

Then all we do is submit the same data as the conditional check on the Tapscript parameter of the Taproot enabled wallet, and the transaction will be valid and posted to the main Bitcoin chain along with the entire contents of the condition data, i.e 'This satoshi is being sent to this address because the data meets the criteria in the conditional check, the data is {data}.'

This gets mined in the next Bitcoin block and the satoshi is then essentially inscribed with the arbitrary data and can be read by any website or app that is capable of reading it.

Initially, people used this new concept to upload data to the Bitcoin blockchain, but remember that there is an upper limit of 4MB in the data (1MB in the main block and 3MB in the extended block), so any file needs to be under 4MB. People uploaded gifs, memes, drawings, even PDF files etc. One of the best I saw in the early batch of ordinals was someone uploaded the entire computer game 'Doom' as a JavaScript executable - if you navigate to that ordinal on a web browser you can literally play the video game directly in your browser from the data that is inscribed onto the Bitcoin blockchain.

Personally, I inscribed an AI generated photograph of my face into a satoshi which now sits on the blockchain forever, you can find it by visiting any ordinals explorer website and searching for ordinal number 208310. Given that the blockchain is downloaded to all nodes, and there are tens of thousands of nodes running the Bitcoin software around the world, there is now a jpeg of my face sitting on tens of thousands of computers around the globe and likely shall remain long after I shuffle off this mortal coil.

In the words of the philosopher Karl Pilkington, 's'abit weird, innit?'

Following on from the use of ordinal inscriptions to store images and files on the Bitcoin blockchain, in March of 2023 we saw the first meaningful deployment of tokens on the Bitcoin chain via the use of what has been called 'BRC-20' contracts deployed to the Bitcoin chain as inscriptions on satoshis via the same method. Deployed by an anonymous contributor named 'Domo' the BRC-20 tokens are named after the same nomenclature that defines most tokens issued on the Ethereum network 'ERC-20' or 'Ethereum Request for Comment - 20' which is the agreed standard by which people are able to generate tokens on the Ethereum network.

Whilst the parallels between the two make it appealing to

draw direct comparisons, there are many differences and the limitations of the amount and complexity of data that can be stored in 4MB blocks bound to individual statoshis limits the functionality that can be utilised on the Bitcoin chain for these tokens. At present only generating, transferring tokens - and the bitcoin blockspace required can make this prohibitively expensive.

Nonetheless, the demand for ordinal inscriptions has driven record levels of activity on the Bitcoin blockchain, as people clamour for blockspace to inscribe their data or generate their shitcoin, which lead to spikes in Bitcoin transaction fees and a long tail list of transactions sitting waiting to get accepted into the next block.

This is good for miners. As the halvings reduce the amount of new bitcoin issued, the fees need to increase in order to financially compensate miners for the work they do and keep the security of the network high by allowing the miners to continue to run large scale operations with incredibly high levels of hashing power. This increased demand for blockspace and competition in the fees paid lead to the first ever instance of blocks in which the fees paid were higher than the new bitcoin rewards of the block, with some blocks in May 2023 having a block reward of 6.25 new bitcoin, but fees of up to 7 bitcoin. This increased demand and increase in fees bodes well for the future security model of bitcoin as the new bitcoin issuance is halved every 4 years.

Despite this, the development of ordinals has, predictably, caused controversy in the Bitcoin community with some factions strongly opposed to them, even going so far as to brand them 'graffiti' or 'vandalism' of the Bitcoin chain. Some call for the ordinal data to be expunged from the chain, or even for those responsible to face sanctions for their actions. Others claim that these are perfectly valid transactions within the rules of the protocol and don't break any rules or laws. Many find themselves somewhere between the two extremes.

Personally, I think that the increase in blockchain usage leading to increased fees is good and builds a model for maintaining the network as bitcoin issuance drops, but also that the ability to spam the network with nonsense bullshit is annoying. Clearly, there is value in being able to store data on a globally distributed, immutable network forever. Humanity probably doesn't benefit that much from me storing a photo on the blockchain, but imagine if people in oppressive regimes used the network to store and access data that is domestically censored. Storing an image of the Tiananmen Square protest 'Tank Man' on the Bitcoin chain puts it immediately beyond the censorship of the Chinese Communist Party, forever. The anonymous nature of the Bitcoin blockchain is such that anyone could now embed documents into the chain, making them immediately public and immutable. I predict we haven't yet seen the main use case of this new development. Imagine if the Watergate documents had been leaked anonymously onto the Bitcoin chain, publicly, or literally any of the WikiLeaks disclosures. A place to publicly share censorship-resistant documents, anonymously and immutably, feels like a tool that has not yet found its best use case.

Whether BRC-20 tokens find market fit or not, the ability to store data on the network isn't going away.

8

Buying, Selling, & Trading Bitcoin

> *"By virtue of exchange, one man's prosperity is beneficial to all others."*
> — Frédéric Bastiat

For most people, their only interaction with Bitcoin is through buying or selling it and being exposed to its price changes. Today, many people hold bitcoin as an investment or as part of a broader investment portfolio. In many ways, Bitcoin is perhaps the most open and egalitarian investment vehicle in the world, given that you can buy as little as a fraction of a penny's worth of bitcoin and that it trades on numerous exchanges across the world.

These inherent properties make it much more accessible than other investment products such as equities, real estate, commodities, etc. Typically, the more common investment vehicles require significant sums of money to invest, and require significant legal and regulatory hurdles to overcome. To invest in real estate requires several thousand dollars of capital to even make a deposit on a property, followed most commonly with a multi-decade mortgage with substantial interest costs, and thousands of dollars in legal fees.

To invest in equity markets, such as buying shares in Amazon or Apple, requires significant documentation to open a licenced trading account, and typically several hundred dollars to purchase a single share, given that most brokers do not allow purchasing fractional shares.

Even physical commodities such as gold face barriers to low-capital investors; despite gold's prevalence and long history as an investment vehicle, even with its widespread network of buyers and sellers, it is still highly impractical to purchase $5 of gold, not to mention the difficulty of verifying you're actually buying gold and not a block of tungsten with a coating of gold.

Anyone, almost anywhere in the world, with an internet connection can buy as little as a few dollars of bitcoin from the comfort of their own home in under an hour. It is little wonder that, despite Bitcoin existing for less than 15 years, and equities markets existing for over 420 years, today in Indonesia there are more people holding cryptocurrencies than holding stocks and shares in companies. In terms of democratising access to investment products, Bitcoin has achieved more in less than 15 years than the entire apparatus of the capitalist investment system has achieved in over four centuries. Aside from anything else, that in and of itself is a remarkable achievement of this nascent technology.

Exchanges

By far the most common way to buy and sell bitcoin is via a cryptocurrency exchange. Crypto exchanges are essentially websites or applications where users can deposit money or cryptocurrencies and trade them with each other, much in the same way a regular stock exchange like the NYSE or LSE does.

Alice creates an account at a crypto exchange and deposits $100. Bob creates an account at the same exchange and deposits 1 bitcoin. Alice places an order to buy 1 bitcoin for $50, and Bob accepts her order; the transaction takes place. The exchange takes a small fee for facilitating the process, and both parties leave happy with their trade. This process takes place millions of times per day, across thousands of exchange platforms worldwide, every minute of every hour of every day. At its core and most basic function, this is how cryptocurrency exchanges work. I have spent the best part of the last decade working as a consultant at or directly with some of the largest cryptocurrencies exchanges in the world (Binance, Pintu, Gemini, Bitget) and seen them grow from small and scrappy startups to multi-billion dollar tech behemoths with valuations bigger than household name companies, influencing political policies across the world. What are they? How do they work? How did we get here in such a short space of time?

Let's unpack the various arms of cryptocurrency exchanges and how they work.

Spot Exchanges

At the most basic core, we have the example above of people buying and selling bitcoin with each other. The same is true of all cryptocurrencies such as Ethereum, Tether, etc., but in this book we will focus solely on Bitcoin. The fact is that almost all exchanges trade in multiple cryptocurrencies, not just bitcoin, in order to increase their user base and revenues, but the core concepts remain the same regardless of the underlying cryptocurrency.

A spot exchange is simply the name given for an exchange that trades the underlying bitcoin—physically, for lack of a better word—between users. Alice buys Bob's bitcoin from him and takes ownership of it; Bob takes Alice's dollars and takes ownership of them. But even in this simple system, there are several ways in which this exchange of money and goods can be facilitated.

Order Books

The most common way in which a trade is facilitated on an exchange is through what is known as the 'order book'. If you've ever seen a market trade, be that equities, crypto, gold, oil, etc. the chances are that what you were looking at was the exchange's 'order book'.

Let's take our above example where Alice has $100 and Bob has 1 bitcoin. Both have funded their exchange accounts with their respective assets and are ready to engage in a trade. How does

Alice know how much bitcoin she will get for the $50 she wants to spend? How does Bob know how many dollars he will get for his 1 bitcoin? Between them, they both need to agree on a price, but they are not in any conversation with each other and, in fact, they don't even know who the other is—nor does it matter.

Both parties are engaging in what is known in financial terms as an 'arm's length' transaction, insofar as both parties are not known to each other and have no personal connection that would affect the price of the trade. This would be distinct from if you were to sell some bitcoin to a friend of yours and give them something of a 'mates rates' deal by chatting together and arriving at a price for them, since you know them.

Exchanges only conduct 'arm's length' trades, so how is the price of the trade arrived at?

Limit Orders - Bid

In order for a trade to take place, one of the parties, Alice or Bob, needs to place an order into the order book of the exchange outlining the size and price of their offering. The order book of an exchange is simply a list of open orders. That is where a user has placed an order to buy or sell a fixed amount of bitcoin at a specified price, these are known as 'limit orders' because you specify the maximum price you are willing to pay to buy or the minimum price you are willing to accept to sell, creating a limit. If we take the example where Alice places an order to buy 1 bitcoin for $50, she types these numbers into the exchange and places her order. This is known as a 'bid' and sits on the bid side of the order book. Alice is bidding to buy 1 bitcoin for $50. This order then sits in the order book for everyone to see that there is an open bid order to buy 1 bitcoin for $50. All orders are shown with their price for a full unit of the bitcoin, even if the offer is for a fraction of a bitcoin.

This order remains in the order book until it is either cancelled by Alice, or until someone sees the bid order and accepts it. Let's say in the above scenario, Bob sees Alice's bid order on the order book and thinks that $50 for his 1 bitcoin is acceptable. Bob can accept that bid, and the matching engine of the exchange will facilitate the trade between Alice and Bob. In this scenario, Alice is known as the 'maker' since she made the market, and Bob is the 'taker' since he took the bid in the market and completed the trade.

Limit Orders - Ask

In the reverse scenario, Bob could have made the market by placing an 'ask' order saying that he is willing to sell 1 bitcoin for $50. In this case, Bob is the 'maker' and when Alice sees his ask offer and accepts it, she becomes the 'taker' when she agrees to his terms of buying 1 bitcoin for her $50.

Typically, exchanges offer a lower fee charged to the person that is the 'maker' than for the 'taker' as the exchange needs to have a full order book in order to attract others to act as the 'taker' and make a trade. Since trades cannot happen without a 'maker' leaving an order sitting in the book waiting for a taker, it is advantageous to encourage maker orders in the book. In some cases, the exchanges waive fees for 'makers' or even offer a fee rebate to users that are the makers in the trade - FTX was a prominent example of this and users could earn fees by being a maker, whilst 'takers' paid a fee for the trade.

In many exchanges, if an order is placed significantly above or below the best available price, the exchange may execute it immediately at the best available price, effectively treating it as a 'market order' for the entire or partial amount, to prevent users from being disadvantaged. In US equities, this follows a rule known as the National Best Bid and Offer (NBBO). For example if Alice had a bid for $50 for 1 bitcoin and, foolishly, Bob placed a limit ask order of $40 for 1 bitcoin, the exchange would simply match his order to Alice's bid and execute the trade at $50 for 1 bitcoin, thus to not unduly disadvantage Bob in his order. Alice is happy as her order gets executed at her desired price/volume and Bob gets a higher price than he was willing to accept.

This is not the case on all exchanges, however, and no legislation exists in cryptocurrency to force this consumer protection rule. Some decentralised exchanges do not enforce this rule and trading on the original Binance DEX for example in the above situation would have seen Bob trade his 1 bitcoin for $40, to Alice's benefit.

Market Orders

The most common way in which a trade is accepted on the 'taker' side of a trade is via what is known as a 'market order'. A market order is when one of the parties only outlines one side of their trade and leaves the other side open, for example, Alice may say 'I want to buy as much bitcoin as I can, right now, instantly, for $50'.

In this type of order, the exchange looks at its open order book and matches Alice's order with the best available ask orders and instantly completes the trade. If the best ask is Bob's 1 for $50 order then the orders match and Alice gets 1 bitcoin for her $50 plus the exchanges fee.

However if the market order is bigger than the best single ask, the order will continue down the order book until the full $50 is completed. For example if the best asks in the market were:

1 bitcoin - $40
0.1 bitcoin - $50
0.1 bitcoin - $50

Alice's market order to buy as much bitcoin as possible for $50 would buy the entire bitcoin from Bob for $40 and then the 0.1 bitcoin from the next two orders at $5 each (0.1 bitcoin at $50 per coin = $5) and she would end up with 1.2 bitcoin for her $50.

Again, this assumes that the exchange acts in its users' best interest and goes through the order book to complete the trade, rather than just matching the best offer and paying Bob $50 for his 1 bitcoin—which is the case for the overwhelming majority of exchanges, but not always.

Market orders get executed immediately and take as much bitcoin as they can for your dollars, or on the other side get as many dollars as they can for your bitcoin. However, as mentioned above, these orders take away open orders on the exchange and reduce the available offers for trade and so typically carry a slightly higher fee as the exchanges usually want to encourage people to fill up their order books.

Bid Ask Spread

At any point in time, there will be a gap between the best ask offer and the best bid offer, because if they overlapped, or even met exactly, then a trade would execute and those orders would disappear from the order book. So at any time there will be a gap between the best available ask and the best available bid, this is known as the 'Bid Ask Spread'.

For example if the only two orders were Bob asking for $55 for 1 bitcoin and Alice bidding $50 for 1 bitcoin, there would be a gap between the two of $5.

Best Ask $55
— Bid-Ask Spread —
Best Bid $50

If another user, Charlie, came in and bid $54 per bitcoin then this spread would then collapse to $1, but since both Charlie's bid and Bob's ask do not meet, no trade will occur.

In today's Bitcoin market, even though bitcoin trades at around $60,000 USD at the time of writing, the market is so active that on many exchanges this bid ask spread is typically a single penny.

Bitcoin Price

The meeting of buyers and sellers in the order books is where the current price of bitcoin is derived from. At any point of time, the current price of bitcoin that is shown prominently on exchanges and other websites is simply the last price at which a trade executed. The most recent price at which a buyer and a seller agreed on a trade is shown as the 'current price', which is why it changes every second, but it is the best way to get a handle on what is the current price at which bitcoin trades at.

Simple Buy - Sell interfaces

Given the potentially daunting interface and multiple order types to pick from on the exchange's order book, many exchanges also offer a much simplified interface from which to buy or sell bitcoin. On Coinbase this is the standard interface and on Binance this is known as the 'One Click Buy Sell' (OCBS) interface. This is perhaps the most commonly used interface for most people to buy bitcoin and essentially just executes a market order on the order book. Customers are presented with a simple interface to buy or sell and then enter in the amount they wish to spend (buy) or the amount of bitcoin to sell (sell) and an indicative price is shown based on the current order book.

Via this user-friendly interface, it's easy to execute a trade and see the balances in your exchange account change (more bitcoin, less cash, or vice versa).

Stablecoins

For many cryptocurrency exchanges, getting reliable access to traditional banking systems has historically been difficult as regulations around the world impose restrictions on digital currencies and platforms that facilitate their trade.
In particular the United States Dollar is quite restricted via a long and boring process of using correspondent banks, which means that any trade with USD essentially has to be routed through the US.

The US government in turn uses its position as a global hegemon to restrict access to US dollars and via these chilling effects, reduce the willingness of banks to work with industries it deems unsavoury. This is not exclusive to cryptocurrency, and has been the bane of many nascent industries such as medicinal cannabis etc. These issues, however, do nothing to stem the demand for US dollars in the cryptocurrency world, both as a means to store value and as a unit against which to trade bitcoin and other cryptocurrencies.

To solve this particular problem, in 2014 the first 'stablecoin' was devised and issued by the company 'Tether'. Initially issued as a cryptocurrency token that piggybacked on the Bitcoin blockchain via something of a layer 2 solution known as the Omni chain, the company began taking USD bank transfer deposits and issuing the equivalent number of USDT tokens to users. The tokens were then seen to be backed 1:1 by USD deposits and could trade in markets as a cryptocurrency asset in place of regular US dollars.

This seemingly small innovation had a substantial impact on the entire cryptocurrency market, allowing US dollars to be sent, received, and traded as native crypto assets entirely bypassing the traditional banking system. For many exchanges this solves the problems with interfacing with the banking systems and allows them to facilitate trade between cryptocurrency assets and US dollars seamlessly. The largest market by daily trade volume for Bitcoin remains the Binance exchange trading pair of bitcoin trading against the USDT synthetic US Dollar digital token.

Back when I first joined Binance in 2018, the exchange operated entirely as a spot exchange between cryptocurrency assets, having no ability to deposit or withdraw traditional currencies such as US dollars. Back in 2018 users were encouraged to purchase USDT stablecoins and then transfer them to Binance in order to trade them for other assets. Even today the many thousands of cryptocurrencies on most exchanges trade against stablecoins rather than actual US Dollars and users are able to deposit and withdraw US Dollar stablecoins in place of actual US Dollars.

The business model of stablecoins is as simple as it is boring, and lucrative; users deposit US dollars to the company and receive US dollar tokens in return. The issuing company then invests the dollars they hold in deposit into low risk investments such as US Government bonds and profit from the interest that these investments pay. If we look at USDT issued by Tether, the current volume of tokens in circulation has ballooned from its 2014 founding to now sit in the region of $84 billion. Given the recent interest hikes in most countries, the company now sits on some $84 billion of deposits that earn in the region of 5% interest in what is known as the 'risk free' market of US Government bonds (They are risk free because the US government will never fail to repay its debt - they would simply print more dollars if needed). As of July 2023, Tether announced their Q2 2023 quarterly profits of $850 million.

There are, of course, many other stablecoins now in the market with the majority focusing on the US dollar. The biggest outside of USDT is USDC, a stablecoin issued by 'Circle' with some $35 billion in circulating supply at time of writing. In addition to this there are also several stablecoins tied to non-USD currencies such as the TGBP, TAUD, THKD, TCAD etc. issued by the company 'Archblock' under the 'True' brand. Binance also issued their own stablecoins with the most prominent being BUSD which hit a peak of almost $24 Billion in circulation before being ordered to shut down by the US government early in 2023. Other regional stablecoins also exist, including a project I worked with in Indonesia called IDRT or Indonesian Rupiah Token. All of whom operate on the same business model.

USDT from Tether has historically attracted significant criticism due to a perceived lack of transparency in their auditing and accounting, which Tether attributes to the difficulty in finding auditors willing and able to work with cryptocurrency companies. However, to date, USDT has never meaningfully 'depegged' or traded below $1, and Tether claims to have processed several billion dollars worth of token redemptions during the period around the collapse of the FTX exchange without any issues. Whilst critics might level allegations that stablecoins are open to abuse, all of the major stablecoin providers retain the ability to freeze funds in users wallets and do so routinely in cases of theft or other illegal activity.

Aside from their use in exchanges for trading, stablecoins are also very commonly used in cross border payments. Personally, I have been paid in stablecoins for the majority of companies I have worked with over the last 5 years. Stablecoins offer a genuine and tangible benefit above the traditional banking system in that I can receive US dollars into my possession in minutes from anywhere in the world without cumbersome and slow traditional banking systems.

For exchanges, stablecoins are a core lifeblood that seamlessly facilitate trade between tokens and traditional currencies whilst avoiding burdensome traditional banking restrictions that have been slow and/or unwilling to adapt to the new reality of digital currencies.

Geographical Arbitrage

Exploiting price differences across various markets is an age-old practice known as arbitrage and remains very popular even in today's advanced financial markets. Arbitrage involves buying an item at a lower price in one market and immediately selling it for a higher price in another market (or selling high and buying back lower). These trades are among the most lucrative an investor can make, as they assume almost zero risk and produce immediate profit.

Infamous rogue trader Nick Leeson exploited price gaps between Asian financial markets before his speculative trades led to the collapse of Barings Bank in 1995 here in Singapore.

These days, in major financial markets, any price gaps between markets are instantly traded away by sophisticated computer trading algorithms, given the small number of highly regulated and advanced markets in which mainstream financial products trade. Given the permissionless nature of Bitcoin, however, there are thousands of exchanges around the globe that allow users to buy and sell Bitcoin with USD or their local currency. Many of these local exchanges typically allow users to trade with their national currency against bitcoin and have banking partnerships to deposit and withdraw that local currency.
In most cases, these local exchanges dominate the domestic market and are the easiest way for people in that country to buy or sell bitcoin which can lead to disconnects from the global price of bitcoin if there is excessive demand in that particular country.

For example, if we imagine that in Indonesia there is a surge in demand for bitcoin, and the local exchanges see large numbers of users wanting to buy bitcoin, this pushes up the selling price as buyers outnumber sellers. If we imagine that in this case bitcoin trades for $10,000 on US exchanges, but in Indonesia the excessive demand has pushed the price up to $11,000 in the local currency. Here we have a potentially perfect geographical arbitrage opportunity to buy bitcoin in the US for $10,000, send it to the Indonesian exchange, and sell it for $11,000, making a

10% profit on the trade for almost no risk.

Provided that you can then quickly and easily withdraw the $11,000 in Indonesian Rupiah and transfer that back to your US bank account, without losing anything on the foreign currency exchange, you could keep running this trade in a loop, extracting profit from the system until the price on the local Indonesian exchange comes back into line with the price on the US exchange.

To facilitate this then, you would need a few things:

1. US Bank account
2. US Bitcoin exchange account
3. Indonesian Bitcoin exchange account
4. Indonesian Bank account
5. Method to quickly and efficiently convert and transfer Indonesian Rupiah to US Dollars

An Indonesian national living in the US would likely have bank accounts in both countries, be able to sign up for exchange accounts in both countries, and have methods for moving Indonesian Rupiah to USD and between countries—and, as a result, could exploit this arbitrage opportunity fairly easily. Ultimately, the people that lose out in the trade are the Indonesian traders who are unable to easily open and fund bitcoin exchange accounts in the US and are forced to pay the higher premium on buying bitcoin on the local Indonesian exchange. The winner in this scenario is the trader who can arbitrage between the US and Indonesian exchanges, bringing the two markets into alignment while profiting from the difference.

Kimchi Premium

Whilst the price gap between Indonesian exchanges and US exchanges has never really been high - currently the difference between bitcoin price on Pintu (Indonesia) and Binance (Global/USD) is around 0.15% - the period between early 2016 and mid 2018 saw a significant disconnect in the price of bitcoin between South Korea and the global USD market price.
This was primarily driven by the factors outlined above, namely a large demand from users in Korea to purchase bitcoin and inability for most global exchanges to process Korean Won.
Over the 2 year period this arbitrage existed, the average price to buy bitcoin in South Korea was 4.80% higher than the global USD average, and hit a peak of 55% in early 2018.

One of the biggest reasons that this gap existed was the South Korean government attempts to dissuade Bitcoin adoption and usage in the country which restricted banks from working with global exchanges; which in turn caused the prices on local Korean exchanges to spike and created the opportunity that was dubbed the 'Kimchi Premium' and allowed foreign trading firms to exploit the demand from local Korean users and extract millions of dollars from the very people the government sought to protect. However, the strict capital controls in place in Korea make the transfer of large sums of money out of the country very difficult and time consuming, which ultimately limited the ability for traders to exploit the trade and explains why the disconnect persisted for so long. Thankfully, the same dynamic was also to be found in the Japanese Bitcoin exchanges and Japan has far fewer restrictions on moving money out of the country.

Among the biggest firms to exploit this trade for profit was Alameda Research, the forerunner to, and ultimately cause of collapse of, the Cryptocurrency exchange FTX.
Alameda Research, the initial hedge fund incorporated by Sam Bankman-Fried, claimed to have made hundreds of millions of dollars in a short space of time by arbitraging the trade between Korean/Japanese exchanges and global USD exchanges. The nascent hedge fund would allegedly have employees lining up at high street banks in Korea and Japan to fill out paper slips to transfer tens of millions of dollars a day back to the US in order for them to run the trade again and extract more value from the arbitrage. Some days, the story goes, the employees would turn up with their pens and find the banks closed for the day or that the transfer window had just closed, resulting in opportunity costs of millions of dollars for the hedge fund.

It's funny now to think that the $32+ Billion powerhouse that was Sam Bankman-Fried and FTX started this way, but given its catastrophic collapse and subsequent allegations of chaotic mismanagement, it does seem pretty fitting.

Ultimately, the fact that Bitcoin is permissionless and censorship-resistant means that governments placing restrictions on their local banking systems and currencies cause these price disconnects and harm domestic users of Bitcoin.

API/Automated trading

Whilst a large amount of the daily trading in bitcoin is done by people buying or selling from their computer or their smart-phone, a substantial amount is traded by automated computers sending buy or sell signals to exchanges without any human intervention. This is also the case in traditional markets as modern technology saw trading move away from smoky trading floors to digital trading platforms, computer science graduates were recruited enmasse to build automated trading algorithms that could detect price movements and then autonomously trade assets in fractions of a second.

A simple example of this might be that you could hold bitcoin and cash balances on trading accounts at two exchanges and monitor the prices on both, if one exchange has a seller looking to sell bitcoin at a price lower than a buyer looking to buy bitcoin on the other exchange, you could have a computer program that detects this and trades on both exchanges - capturing that arbitrage without needing to move bitcoin or money between the two exchanges.

Another idea might be to write a computer script that checks Elon Musk's Twitter feed every second to detect a new tweet mentioning Bitcoin. If one is found, the script could immediately use your account's entire cash balance to purchase Bitcoin and then sell it one hour later. Assuming, as is often the case, Elon's tweet sends the price of bitcoin skyrocketing, this would be a profitable trade and your automated trading code would be sitting ready to execute this 24/7, even when you are asleep.

There are many various ideas you could think of that could be used to build automated trading systems. Personally, I built and ran several on FTX.com, with varying degrees of success.

Recently, exchanges have begun rolling out the ability for users to program automated trading bots directly on the exchange by following simple to use on screen builders, but these are limited to the data the exchange has - for example they would not be able to monitor Elon's tweets. But historically this was all done by writing code that you host on the internet somewhere and connecting to your exchange account using what is know as an API (Application Programming Interface). These API's are simply systems built by the exchange that allow external code to talk to the exchange and process requests to execute commands on behalf of the user that is making them.
Most modern Bitcoin exchanges have APIs and all work broadly the same:
The user generates an API key or keys within the exchange which the code will use instead of the username and password, then your code runs and passes a message to the exchange via the API and passes your API keys to identify you are the user making the request. If the request is valid and your keys match the keys you generated when you set up your API account, then the orders you sent are executed and any trades are made.

Whilst these interfaces are mostly used by big trading firms, it's still popular and viable to code your own bots up to utilise the APIs on exchanges to suit your needs. For example on FTX I built a simple bot that would take my monthly salary deposit and lend out 90% of the USD to earn interest, but then also make incremental purchases of bitcoin every 20 minutes to slowly build up my bitcoin holdings by 'Dollar Cost Averaging' my entry price into the market. Without missing a beat, every 20 minutes of every day the code would scoop up a little more bitcoin.

Market Makers

The tricky thing with exchanges is that nobody wants to trade on an exchange that has no trading volume, because the gap between the bid and ask can be very large and the amount of time it would take to get your order filled can be significant.

If there are few buyers and few sellers, the gaps between them can be large and the volume of trade then is low and slow. To some degree this is mitigated in very liquid and fungible assets such as bitcoin by people arbitraging the asset between exchanges; if your exchange has a person looking to sell for $10 and another exchange has a buyer looking to buy at $11 then someone could swoop in and take both of those trades and pocket a dollar in arbitrage. However, having few buyers and sellers and the low volume this leads to can make these opportunities not worth the time and hassle for the arbitrager to deal with the associated overheads. Even if the price gap is large, if the volume of bitcoin for sale is low, this can render such a trade more trouble than it is worth. On the opposite side of this, liquidity begets liquidity. If your exchange has substantial volume already then it will attract more volume of trade simply because of that liquidity, which creates a snowball effect that increases the liquidity of your exchange.

For this reason, most exchanges employ the services of dedicated teams, known as 'market makers' to keep the order books of the exchange filled with both buy and sell orders that give prospective customers orders to buy or sell into. Market makers sit on an exchange and populate both sides of the order book to reduce the gap between the buy and sell side and provide depth in the order book using API and algorithms to monitor and add or remove bids and asks depending on the price movement of the asset, and also seek to hedge their positions via other trading products in order not to get caught on the wrong side of large price movements and lose money, or to profit from correctly buying and selling the asset and the price of it moves up and down over time. Most commonly this is a paid service that the exchange, or token project will pay a third party to provide, which allows the market maker to keep the markets tight and liquid around the price of an asset rather than seek to profit directly from trading the asset, which would conflict with the goal of keeping the market tightly priced.

This is more common on other cryptocurrencies, also known as 'shitcoins', given the fact that they often trade on very few exchanges and have inherently low demand to buy or sell them. In my experience in consulting and working with shitcoin projects, most exchanges require the projects to engage a market maker service - or simply provide fee free trading to the project to trade back and forth with themselves to give the illusion of volume and liquidity; some exchanges even mandate that the project must trade a specific volume of the token back and forth with themselves every day in an exercise that is known as 'painting the tape' - a practice that is illegal in most regulated asset markets when it is done to artificially manipulate the price of an asset.

A common recent example of this could, potentially, have been seen during the collapse of FTX with the price of their FTT token. As problems arose and the wheels began to come off of the exchange, the price of the FTT token nosedived; it was clear from the order book in FTX that someone, or group of people/entities were 'defending' the price of the token at $22 per token. As more pressure piled on the selling pressure against the token rose and rose and speculators saw an opportunity to short sell the token or take leveraged derivative positions against it, profiting if the price fell significantly.

Eventually, at some point, the market maker or makers that were defending the $22 price ran out of money and were unable to continue absorbing the increasing amount of tokens that wanted to sell at the $22 price and the price rapidly fell to $4. For reasons not relevant to this book, someone had a significant interest in keeping the price of that shitcoin above $22 and threw everything but the kitchen sink at it, but once they ran out of money and the market was able to accurately price it, it collapsed.

When done legitimately on high liquidity assets like bitcoin, however, market making is broadly seen as a necessary good in order to keep markets efficient and pricing tight to avoid large gaps between buyers and sellers that can harm retail traders.

Visa Cards

A common criticism of bitcoin is that it is not useful in the real world and can't be spent or used in the real world. This gave rise to the old joke:

A guy is in a bar and walks up to two attractive ladies, he says; 'I'm a bitcoin millionaire!'
The ladies say: 'That's great, do you want to buy us a drink?'
The guy sheepishly replies: 'Oh, sorry, I don't have any real money' and slopes off.

The joke touches on a very real point: bitcoin is of little use if it can't be used to buy goods or services in the real world. Given that your local bar is unlikely to accept bitcoin yet, many exchanges have sought to bridge this gap by issuing their own Visa or Mastercards. These cards allow users to spend their Bitcoin anywhere Visa or Mastercard are accepted.

These typically fall into two types, either dynamically selling your bitcoin at the moment you make a purchase on your card, or allowing you to pre-load your card with fiat currency by selling your bitcoin in advance.

This was a significant step in integrating the Bitcoin world and the real economy and removing the need to go through a longer process of selling bitcoin, moving the money back to your bank account and then spending it. Particularly as the traditional financial world has implemented barriers between banking systems and the Bitcoin world in recent years, often cutting off or heavily restricting the ability to move money between bank accounts and Bitcoin exchanges.

I was one of the first customers of the exchange Crypto.com (formerly Monaco) to get a Visa card attached to my account. For a three-year period between 2018 and 2021, I genuinely lived without a bank account. My employer at the time was Binance, the cryptocurrency exchange, which paid me directly into my exchange account in their own cryptocurrency, BNB (formerly Binance Coin). I would trade BNB for bitcoin and transfer it to my Crypto.com account. From there, I could sell the bitcoin for Singapore dollars loaded directly onto my Visa card. For the majority of 2020, I was stranded in Bali due to the COVID-19 travel restrictions and lived entirely from my Visa card powered by bitcoin. I rented accommodation via Airbnb using the card, covered my cost of living, and, where required, withdrew Indonesian Rupiah directly from an ATM to get physical cash for places that did not accept Visa cards.

Today, many exchanges and other companies offer Visa or Mastercards that are powered by bitcoin or other cryptocurrencies in this way.

On the back end of this is a simple exchange mechanism to take your bitcoin and match it with a buyer either on their own exchange, via a market maker, or routing to another exchange and crediting your Visa or Mastercard with the resulting fiat currency.

Crypto.com were arguably the first and most successful to launch this program, but were followed by several of the other big exchanges, notably Binance and Coinbase.

This final bridge between the Bitcoin world and the real world meant that it was now entirely possible to send real-world currency to anyone, anywhere in the world, in minutes, which they could withdraw from any ATM.
In 2020, during the COVID-19 restrictions, I found myself on a small island in the Lombok Strait at 10p.m. on a Sunday night, long after the last boat had left. The card processing facilities of the island were not working. Unable to pay for our accommodation and facing the prospect of several days without any money, I leveraged the permissionless and immutable Bitcoin network to transfer bitcoin to my Visa card, withdraw cash from a local ATM, and avert a crisis.

Whilst many of these cards still work and function well, there have been disruptions and failures; all of which have been from the traditional banking sector.

The Crypto.com card was issued and facilitated by Wirecard, which collapsed overnight in spectacular fashion under the weight of massive corruption and fraud in June 2020. This left millions of Crypto.com card users locked out of their cards until continuation solutions were found. My Coinbase card, along with many other users, continued to be arbitrarily frozen until I gave up on trying to use it. Other companies that offered Crypto powered cards, such as TenX, collapsed or ran into regulatory hurdles they were unable to surmount.

Whilst I still use my Crypto.com card today, it has significant problems and is no longer suitable to use as my only card. Such things are perhaps to be expected when operating on the fringes of a new technological frontier. However, bitcoin powered Visa and Mastercards are certainly here to stay and I have no doubt that in time they will become a lot more stable, common, and widespread.

Yield Earning Programs

One of the more controversial business areas in Bitcoin and crypto in the early 2020s was certainly the various platforms that offered users a yield income on their bitcoin or crypto. There were many such platforms from around 2018; however by the end of 2022 almost all had gone bankrupt or massively cut back their offerings. These platforms played a significant role in the market collapse of 2021-2022 and the implosion of the big names that went against the wall in that cycle, including FTX and 3AC.

In most cases, the platforms took on client deposits in bitcoin or crypto and then utilised them in some way to generate more money and passed part of that on to their user base in the form of a yield. Sometimes this yield was gained by executing complex derivatives trades - such as the 'carry trade' on derivatives exchanges; but in many cases the yield was achieved by lending out the underlying assets to crypto hedge funds who would execute their own complex trades and return a premium to the lenders.

The GBTC Premium Arbitrage

The most famous of these was the GBTC premium arbitrage trade that the Singapore based Hedge Fund 3 Arrows Capital (3AC) executed.

Essentially, the inability and inaction of global government regulatory bodies to understand and embrace Bitcoin created the circumstances that resulted in millions of honest retail users losing billions of dollars of their hard earned money.
For over a decade, the SEC in the United States have continued to deny any bitcoin tracking ETF approval to list in the US stock markets, giving increasingly incoherent and ridiculous justifications. This lead to a gap in the market where there is a clear demand to access exposure to bitcoin via the regulated markets in the US but no product to fill that demand.

In came the Grayscale Open Ended Trust which, whilst not quite an ETF, was able to trade on the New York stock exchanges very similar to an ETF and holds bitcoin as its underlying asset. The fund would later converted to an ETF following regulatory approval in January 2024.

With huge demand for Bitcoin on the regulated market and only one product available, the demand quickly overwhelmed the supply and drove the price of the GBTC product on the stock market to trade as high as 50% above its underlying value.

The mechanism for creating new GBTC shares was as follows:

Send in your bitcoin.

Get given GBTC shares equal to the value of your bitcoin.
After 6 months, the shares are released and you can sell them for US dollars.

If you had 100 bitcoin, you could deliver them to Grayscale, get 100 bitcoin worth of GBTC shares, then 6 months later (assuming the GBTC still trades at 50% above the underlying value) sell the shares for 150 bitcoin worth of US dollars.

You could then buy 150 bitcoin and send them through the system again and get 225 bitcoin out the other side in 6 months.

3AC saw this trade and began to borrow as much bitcoin as they could from any possible source. If they could generate 125% returns on bitcoin in a year, they could easily offer 10% yield to anyone to borrow their bitcoin and then use them to execute this trade and pocket a healthy 110% return on the borrowed bitcoin.

The problem here, of course, is that collecting billions of dollars of bitcoin from the disparate public is tricky, and holding millions of counterparts is troublesome.
Much better then if they could simply reach out to platforms that already held billions of dollars of retail customers bitcoin and make a deal with them as 1-1 entities to borrow the underlying bitcoin that belonged to users, in return for a share of the profit from their exotic trade.

So it came to be that 3AC ended up borrowing billions of dollars of client funds from the major yield earning programs such as Celsius, BlockFi, Genesis, etc.

Unfortunately, in February 2021 this trade started to unwind and the GBTC shares on the New York stock exchange began to trade at a discount to their underlying bitcoin. Rather than making a profit on this trade now, 3AC would get back less money than they owed to the people they had borrowed the bitcoin from. This happened as interest in Bitcoin among Wall Street disappeared and other competing funds became available.

At its peak, the discount on the GBTC shares vs the underlying bitcoin was almost -49%, meaning 100 bitcoin in would get only 51 bitcoin out the other side in 6 months time.

In June 2022, 3AC was already significantly impacted by the collapse of the Luna/Terra protocol and suffered substantial losses. The collapse of the GBTC trade also inflicted substantial losses on the fund causing it to collapse. Billions of dollars of bitcoin remain unpaid to users. The knock on effect took down many of the main yield earning platforms and ultimately starting the collapse of the exchange FTX which lead to further knock on collapses.

Many lawsuits continue through the courts today across the world, at time of writing, the CEO of 3AC, Su Zhu has been released from a Singapore prison cell, while the CEO of FTX, SBF will remain in a federal prison for more than two decades, and others are still fighting significant legal battles. Almost all yield earning platforms have disappeared from the cryptocurrency space, or those that have remained have dramatically cut their interest rates and maximum investment limits.

In the case of Genesis (A crypto hedge fund), the situation

appears even murkier as the company appears to have borrowed bitcoin from Gemini (A crypto exchange) users and then executed the GBTC trade - however GBTC is issued by Grayscale and a sister company of Genesis, both under the DCG (Digital Currency Group) with allegations of moral hazard that may have arisen from using external users funds to swell the proceeds of their sister company. This matter is currently being pursued in court and Gemini retail users remain out of pocket.

It does make one think, if the SEC had simply approved a Bitcoin ETF, there would have been no premium on GBTC and nothing to arbitrage. There would be no huge incentive to borrow funds from retail investors to throw at the trade, and ultimately it would have saved millions of everyday people from suffering tens of billions of dollars of losses. Whilst there are a lot of bad actors in this sad story, the SEC itself carries a large share of blame for its obstinance with Bitcoin.

Crypto.com

One notable and prominent player that avoided exposure to the GBTC trade and 3AC fall out was Crypto.com. Having used Crypto.com extensively from 2018 until 2022, the yield earning facility was pretty incredible. The offer was to earn 8% on your Bitcoin up to a maximum of $1 million of bitcoin, if you locked it up for 3 months with them.

The limitation on the $1 million ceiling was calculated based on current US dollar value of bitcoin and at the point of adding more bitcoin to the program. This meant that if bitcoin was at

$40k and you had 25 Bitcoin in the program, you were at the limit and could add no more. If the price of Bitcoin dropped to $38,400 you could add another Bitcoin to the program as the total balance would then still be below $1 million, but if the price went back up to $40k you would be earning 8% on the entire $1.04 million.

It's crazy to think now, but as I lounged around my villa in Bali during the COVID 2020 lockdowns I would check the app every day trying to squeeze more bitcoin in under the limit, and earning $7k a month in interest.
Those days are gone and are never coming back—a product of the COVID-19 monetary policies and zero interest rate environment.

Crypto.com avoided any exposure to 3AC or the GBTC trade and reportedly ran these programs as a loss leader program to encourage new sign ups.

As of today, the interest rate offered is 1.25% on Bitcoin, with a maximum allocation of $3,000.

Non-Custodial Exchanges

The final digital venue on which bitcoin can be exchanged is via platforms known as non-custodial exchanges. As the name implies these are exchanges where you retain direct ownership of your bitcoin, rather than sending them into an exchange platform and giving up direct ownership of it. Given the limitations of the Bitcoin blockchain, these do not exist directly on the Bitcoin chain and require using a wrapped bitcoin solution that we mentioned in previous chapters. Whilst some non-custodial exchanges do exist on some sidechains of Bitcoin, the majority exist on Ethereum and other native smart contract enabled chains.

In recent years non-custodial exchanges have become very big on the Ethereum chain using what are known as Automated Market Makers (AMM). With wrapped bitcoin on the Ethereum chain it would be possible to buy or sell bitcoin via an AMM.

How these AMMs work is quite simple:

Someone creates a pair for trading on the AMM by placing both sides of the trade into a 'pool' which establishes the initial trading price.

For example if I wanted to create a pool for bitcoin and USDC (A US dollar stablecoin), and the current price of bitcoin was $1,000 I might fund a pool with 100 bitcoin and $100,000 of USDC.

If someone wishes to buy bitcoin from the pool they might send $1,000 into the pool and receive 1 bitcoin out of the pool, this would leave a pool with 99 bitcoin and $101,000 in USDC which would then cause the price of bitcoin in the pool to reprice to $101,000 / 99 bitcoin making the price $1,020.20 per bitcoin. This is to be expected as more purchasing demand raises the price.
The same applies in reverse if a person sells a bitcoin into the pool and the price of the bitcoin would fall the respective amount.

If the price of the pool moves further than the market price of bitcoin, it creates a financial incentive for someone to arbitrage trade the AMM to bring the price back into line with the market price, and keeps the AMM price in line with the rest of the market.

The advantages of AMMs and other non-custodial exchanges are that you retain control of your assets at all times and don't give up control of your coins, but also that you are able to trade without providing KYC documentation that reveals your identity.

Whilst AMMs are very popular in the broader crypto space, they remain seldom used in Bitcoin, due to the requirement to wrap/unwrap your bitcoin onto another chain in order to use them.

OTC & P2P

The final main method for buying or selling bitcoin is through peer to peer trades directly with a counterparty. These can either be facilitated by exchanges, by chat groups or mailing lists, or via institutions using Over the Counter (OTC) trades. In any case the trades are offered or advertised by one side and accepted by the counterparty and then the method of transfer for the money is agreed directly by the two parties. Occasionally, where required, the parties may opt to use an escrow to take hold of the money and the bitcoin and then release either side to their owners only when both sides have given up control of them to the counterparty or the escrow.

In Singapore, and I assume in other large cities, there is an active peer-to-peer trading market where traders offer up trades and other traders accept them. These are frequently conducted on a cash basis with people meeting in person and handing over bags of cash in return for the bitcoin being released to the buyer.

When transacting at a large size, it can be preferable to execute that trade directly with an institution using an OTC trade in order to prevent the large trade size significantly moving the price of bitcoin. These OTC trades are facilitated by dedicated trading companies that hold large quantities of both bitcoin and money and will offer a price to you based on your intended trade size, then seek to trade in the open market to backfill your trade into their inventory. Given that these OTC trades are designed for large size orders, many OTC desks have minimum size requirements in order to facilitate a trade, typically $50,000 or more.

9

Bitcoin Derivatives Trading

> *"My partner Charlie says there is only three ways a smart person can go broke: liquor, ladies and leverage. Now the truth is — the first two he just added because they started with L — it's leverage."*
> — Warren Buffett

Derivatives are financial instruments or contracts that get their value from the price of an underlying asset. Explained in another way, their value derives from the price of another asset, hence the name 'derivatives' or 'derivatives contracts'. The most common types of derivatives contracts in the Bitcoin and crypto space are 'futures contracts' and 'options contracts', both of which we will cover in this section.

Futures Contracts

Whilst some evidence exists to point to the existence of Futures Contracts as far back as 4 BC in Ancient Greek olive markets, the first documented and verifiable existence of futures contract trading can be traced back to 17th Century Japan. The Dojima Rice Exchange in Osaka was established in 1697 as the first ever known formal futures contract trading venue.

So, what is a futures contract?

Japanese Rice Farmers

Well, as the name implies, it is a contract relating to the future. Let's take the Japanese rice farmers as an example for our explanation:

Let's say you are a rice farmer in 17th century Japan and you plant enough rice to harvest 100 standard bags of rice in the harvest time in 6 months' time. Now, you know the cost to produce your bag of rice is 100 yen, but the sale price that you can get for the bag of rice varies greatly depending on the harvest.

If the summer weather is good, many people will choose to grow rice in their own fields, and at harvest time there will be much more rice available and reduced demand. In this case, a bag of rice would sell for 120 yen.

If the summer weather is very bad, nobody will be able to grow rice aside from dedicated farmers, and even some of those will fail, in that case at the harvest time there will be an undersupply of rice and increased demand and a bag of rice could sell for 300 yen.

How much you can sell your rice for varies drastically depending on factors outside of your control and could lead to bumper profits or operating losses.

Now, imagine there is a chef in your town who needs to buy 100 bags of rice every year for his restaurant. He is faced with the opposite problem as you but the same volatility. If the weather is good, he can buy rice cheaply; if it is bad he has to fork out a lot for the rice.

Now, imagine the chef comes to you at the start of the season when you are planting your rice and proposes the following trade contract:

'I promise to buy your rice from you, at the harvest date, for 200 yen per bag, regardless of the market price'

This means that if the weather is great, you're still able to sell your bags at 200 yen rather than 120 yen, but in return if the weather is bad you only get 200 yen per bag vs 300 yen per bag you would otherwise receive.

For the chef, he equally locks in his price and saves money if it's a bad summer but takes a loss if the summer is good.

Both parties benefit from the price security here. You are able to invest more into next year's harvest by knowing you will get

200 per bag at harvest and can spend more next year without having to fear you might only get 120 per bag.
The Chef can take pre-bookings for his restaurant knowing that he can make as many meals as his budget can handle at 200 yen per bag and wont end up unable to deliver if the price at harvest was 300 yen per bag.

That is the basic concept of a futures contract, it contains 3 key elements:

1. Amount (How much stuff are you agreeing to buy?)
2. Strike Price (At what price?)
3. Strike Date (When?)

Cash Settled Futures

Now, there are essentially two ways in which a futures contract can be settled, either 'physically settled' or 'cash settled'.

Physically settled is easy enough to understand, in the contract above the chef takes physical delivery of the rice and pays you 200 yen per bag.

Cash settlement would be helpful for both sides, for example, if the price of rice was trading at 150 yen per bag but the chef has a farmer next to him that will sell him rice at 150 yen and you have a buyer next to you that will buy at 150 yen per bag, the contract could be settled in the following way:

Both sides agree that selling/buying with their neighbour is easier, but since the agreement was to buy from you at 200 yen per bag, the chef agrees to send you 50 yen per bag for the 100 agreed bags (5,000 yen). That way, you sell your rice to your neighbor for 15,000 yen but get 5,000 yen from the chef under the futures contract, making a total of 20,000 yen for the 100 bags. The chef buys rice locally for 15,000 yen but sends you 5,000 yen, giving a total outlay of 20,000 yen for 100 bags of rice. The contract settles without the need for physical delivery of the rice from you to the chef, making the whole process easier and cheaper, as transferring money between parties is much quicker and simpler than moving 100 bags of rice.

Now if we just transport that same concept forward in time some 330 years and transpose it over Bitcoin, we get the concept of Bitcoin futures trading with cash settled contracts.

I might choose to buy (known as a 'long contract', 'longing', or 'going long') a Bitcoin futures contract for 1st January 2025 for a size of 1 bitcoin and a price of $45,000.
On the 1st of January, at the settlement date, if the price of bitcoin is $35,000 then I pay you $10,000 as I agreed to buy it from you at $45,000 and the difference between my promise and the market price is -$10,000.
If at the time of settlement, the market price is $55,000 then you pay me $10,000 as the market price is +$10,000 above our agreed price.

Now, if between now and the 1st of January 2025 the price of bitcoin rises, and the price that people are trading futures contracts for the 1st of January rises to $50,000, I could choose to accept a trade offer to sell 1 bitcoin for $50,000 on the 1st of

January. Then my exposure to the market is flat because:

1. I have an agreement to buy 1 Bitcoin from you for $45,000.

2. I have an agreement to sell 1 Bitcoin to another person for $50,000.

Regardless of the price of Bitcoin now, I have locked in a confirmed buy and sell price and I make $5,000 in profit.
I do not need to close out my futures contract with you; I can always close out the other side of the contract with anyone trading in the market and fulfill my open obligation to buy from you by offloading that to another person who agrees to buy from me.

So what is the advantage of trading futures and why are they so popular in Bitcoin?

Futures contracts dwarf 'spot' purchases of actual bitcoin by orders of magnitude, which is essentially due to one very simple reason: leverage.

To understand this, we need to first understand what 'liquidations' are and what it means to be 'liquidated'.

So, let's say you have $10,000 on your exchange trading account and 1 bitcoin is trading for $40,000. Your $10,000 can buy you 0.25 bitcoin, and if the price of 1 bitcoin rises to $50,000 then your 0.25 bitcoin is worth $12,500 and you profit by $2,500.

If you decide to trade bitcoin futures, you don't need the full $40,000 in order to buy exposure to 1 full bitcoin, so you could enter a futures contract to buy 1 bitcoin on the 1st January 2025 for $40,000. If the price rises to $50,000 then you are in profit $10,000 and the other party of the contract pays you $10,000.

In both cases, bitcoin rose from $40,000 to $50,000 and you only ever invested $10,000, but by using futures you made a 100% return on investment, versus 25% if you had just purchased spot bitcoin.

So, why is that? This is because of leverage. Let's examine what would happen if the price moved against you and traded down instead of up.

Liquidations

If the price, instead of trading up to $55,000, moved down to $35,000, then the 0.25 Bitcoin you purchased on spot would still be yours in your wallet but would be worth $8,750. Hopefully, if you hold on to it and it comes back later to $55,000, it would then be worth $13,750, and you'd be in profit again.

However, if you used the $10,000 as collateral to open a futures trade, things would have gone quite differently.

The contract commits you to purchase 1 bitcoin on the agreed date for $45,000, but as the price moves down, the amount that you owe your counterparty increases.

If 1 bitcoin were to trade at $40,000, then you would owe your counterparty $5,000 as the cash settlement portion of your agreement. This is because he is only able to sell 1 bitcoin for $40,000, but you agreed to buy it for $45,000, leaving a $5,000 gap that you must cover.

Now, if the price fell further before the settlement date, and hit $36,000, at this point $9,000 of your $10,000 balance is owed to the counterparty and the exchange that you trade on needs to take steps to ensure that you don't run up debts bigger than you are able to pay.

It is around this point that you would likely be hit with the dreaded 'margin call,' where the exchange would email you to request that you deposit more funds into your account, as your available balance to cover potential losses is getting low.

If you add more funds, your trade will stay open, and the exchange is assured that you have enough money to cover your potential losses even if the price falls further.

However, if you do not add more funds and the trade continues to move against you, the exchange will, at some point, close your open position by selling your obligation to buy from the counterparty to someone else in the market at the current market price, closing you out of your obligations.

If, for example, this happened at a $35,000 price, then you would have agreed to buy from one person at $45,000 and agreed to sell to another at $35,000. Your entire $10,000 would be gone to cover the gap between those two obligations.

This is known as getting 'liquidated,' and you are then left with nothing in your account, as your entire $10,000 is used to cover your contractual obligations.

Trading futures allows you to leverage up your funds to get more price exposure, but that comes with amplified losses if the trade goes against you. There is no such thing as a free lunch, not in this game.

For the most part, most average retail users should probably not fuck around with futures or leverage. Over the last 6 years I made millions of dollars buying Bitcoin, but the only way I ever lost millions of dollars in a single day was with leveraged futures.

BitMEX Perpetual Futures

One of the leading examples of innovation in the financial world that has been built on top of Bitcoin is possibly the development of what are known as 'perpetual futures' contracts.

First proposed by the Nobel Prize winning economomist, Robert Shiller, in 1992, perpetual futures contracts are futures contracts that abstract away the need for a strike date and continuously roll over the open contracts into the future in perpetuity.

Unlike dated futures, there is no settlement date when the price of the futures contract is forced to reconcile with the underlying price of the asset.
This can cause the price of the futures contract to drift above

or below the current price of the underlying asset and stay disconnected for a while.

With a dated future, cash-settled, the price of the contract settles at the underlying price of the asset at the date of settlement. If the contracts are settling long in the future, it's normal for them to be above the current price of the asset; for example, a bitcoin futures contract settling a year from now may well trade at several percentage points above the current price, implying that the market expects the price to rise by a similar amount in that period.

As an example, the furthest dated Bitcoin future that I can find today on Deribit (a derivatives exchange) is trading at $65,313 which is 8.06% above the current bitcoin price of $60,413.

On the date of settlement the contract will close exactly at the spot price of the underlying so there is no need for any mechanism to force the price of the futures contract to align with the underlying asset, as the settlement date handles that. Accordingly, the gap between shorter dated futures is smaller, as time left to settlement is less. The January futures on Deribit currently trades at 1.69% above the underlying.

The lack of a settlement date on perpetual futures presents a problem of how to keep the futures contract price in line with the underlying price. As with any traded product, the price is simply a reflection of supply and demand, and in periods of irrational exuberance, the price can float significantly higher, or, in periods of fear, drift lower. This is because, if you anticipate a substantial rise or fall in the price of bitcoin, you can utilise the leverage of futures contracts to make outsized profits, as explained earlier in the section on leverage trading.

To address this, perpetual futures contracts utilise a system of 'funding periods' and 'funding rates' to force the price to align with the underlying price of the asset.

The funding period is simply a fixed rolling timeframe. On BitMEX, that is every eight hours, but other platforms have different periods. These periods, in effect, act as micro settlements without closing out the contract, in the following way.

If the current price of the perpetual futures contract is above the price of the underlying asset, anyone who is 'long' (purchased a contract) pays a small fee to the side that is 'short' (sold a contract). Conversely, if the price of the perpetual futures contract is below the price of the underlying asset, then the flow of payment is reversed ('shorts' pay to 'longs'). The value of this payment is dependent on how far away from the underlying price the perpetual futures price is.

For example if the perpetual futures price is only 0.1% above the underlying price of bitcoin then anyone that is holding a 'long' contract will pay a small fee to anyone that is 'short' every 8 hours, but if the market is going crazy and the anticipation of price rise is high so that the perpetual futures price is trading 5% above the underlying price, then the fee paid from 'longs' to 'shorts' will be substantial.

This acts as a method of damping exuberance in either direction, as the fees paid to maintain the gap between the perpetual futures price and the underlying become prohibitive when the ongoing fee to keep your 'long' or 'short' contract open grows substantial. This means either the price of the underlying asset needs to move in the direction of the perpetual future to reduce the ongoing fees paid, or traders will start to close their contracts, which will drive the price of the perpetual future back into line with the underlying asset.

The Carry Trade

An ingenious consequence of this system is that it gives rise to the ideal trading opportunity: a risk-free reward trade that can be executed.

If the hype in the market is high and the price of the perpetual future climbs significantly above the underlying price of bitcoin, it's intuitive to think, 'Why would anyone want to take the other side of that trade?'—if the whole market is strongly implying that the price is set to rise, surely betting against that is a silly move. The same is, of course, true in the opposite direction, but for the sake of simplicity in this explanation, we will stick to a case where the price detaches to the upside and trades significantly above the price of bitcoin.

For example:

The perpetual futures contract price trades at 5% above the price of bitcoin.
The funding rate on the exchange is currently 0.05% every eight hours.
If we work out the funding on an annualised basis, we simply

take the funding rate of 0.05% and multiply it by three to get the 24-hour rate, and then by 365.25 to get the annual rate:

0.05% x 3 x 365.25 = 54.79%

That means that on an annualised basis, if you were to 'short' the futures contract you would receive 54.79% return on your investment.

However, if the price of bitcoin goes up, then you will incur losses, as you agreed to sell your bitcoin at that price and now it's worth more. When you close out your perpetual futures contract, you will be forced to pay the difference between the new higher price and the price you agreed to sell your futures contract at.

What would be good, then, is if you could hedge your bitcoin price risk and execute this trade so that you capture that 54.79% premium but are not exposed to the change in the price of bitcoin.

You can't hedge your exposure here by 'longing' the contract, as you'd then simply be taking both sides of the trade and paying the 54.79% on one side and capturing it on the other, making your position net flat. However, if you simply hold the underlying bitcoin in the same volume that you 'short' the perpetual futures, your exposure to the bitcoin price is neutral, and you can simply collect the 54.79% funding rate.

This creates an absolutely risk-free trade and allows you to achieve a favourable return on investment without being exposed to the bitcoin price.

Let's run a quick example to illustrate this.

You have $50,000 to invest.
You purchase 1 bitcoin for $50,000.
The bitcoin perpetual futures contract trades at 5% above spot at $52,500.
The funding rate is 0.05% every eight hours.
You short the perpetual futures contract at $52,500.

A week later, the price of bitcoin is $60,000
The perpetual futures contract still trades $2,500 above the spot price at $62,500
The funding rate is 0.04%

Your 1 bitcoin is now worth $60,000, a profit of $10,000 ($60,000 - $50,000)
Your perpetual futures contract is now at a loss of -$10,000 ($62,500 - $52,500)
You collected 7 days of funding of 0.05% every 8 hours
(7 x 0.05% x 3) x $55,000* = $557.50

** For simple mathematics we calculate the funding payments as if the price were*

$55,00 for the entire week

- an average between $50,000 - $60,000

Total:

1 bitcoin = + $10,000
Perp contract = - $10,000
Funding = +$557.50

= \$557.50
=1.115% (57.79% on an annualised basis)

Provided you sell the perpetual futures contract when it is above the underlying price, and close the contract before its price falls below the underlying bitcoin price, the value of your bitcoin is fully hedged by the spot bitcoin you hold, and you have collected the funding payments risk-free.

The same trade is possible with dated futures and is much simpler. If the futures contract for a year from now is trading at \$55,000 and the spot price today is \$50,000, you can simply buy 1 bitcoin and sell the futures contract at \$55,000. When the contract closes in a year's time, you will lock in a \$5,000 profit.

For example, in a year's time if the price of bitcoin is \$100,000

1 bitcoin = (\$100,000 - \$50,000) = + \$50,000
Futures contract = (\$55,000 - \$100,000) = - \$45,000
= +\$5,000

If, instead, in a year's time the price of bitcoin is \$10,000

1 bitcoin = (\$10,000 - \$50,000) = - \$40,000
Futures contract = (\$55,000 - \$10,000) = + \$45,000
= +\$5,000

All of these futures carry trades are risk-free arbitrage trades that help keep the price of the futures contracts in line with the underlying price, either via the settlement date or the funding rate payments. These methods give large institutional funds, which seek to trade profitably in the markets without taking any exposure to the underlying volatility of the price of bitcoin, ways to trade in the market and provide stability and liquidity to bitcoin speculators.

CME

Finally, on futures, the Chicago Mercantile Exchange (CME) is the largest futures contract exchange globally and launched bitcoin futures contracts in December 2017. This exchange is a fully legitimate and accredited institutional exchange in the US and frequently trades over a billion dollars of contracts each month. This provides a venue for regulated institutions in the US to execute trades on a regulated exchange, gaining exposure to the price of bitcoin.

Options

The final type of derivatives contract that exists in the bitcoin world is the 'options contract'. Now that we have done the heavy lifting of understanding futures contracts, options are easier to comprehend.

Essentially, options contracts are simply futures contracts without the obligation to execute—hence the name 'options'.

An options contract contains four key components:

Quantity

Strike price
Strike date
Premium

The quantity, strike date, and price are the same as in a futures contract:
I want to buy **x** bitcoin on **y** date for **z** price.

The difference here, though, lies in the optionality of executing the contract and the premium fee you either pay to buy it or receive to sell it.
The benefit in this is that if the trade goes against you, you can simply choose not to execute the contract and you do not bear all of the losses that you would be on the hook for in order to settle your futures contract. For this optionality, you pay a fee to the seller, and in the case that your trade goes against you, your losses are limited to the amount you paid to buy the contract.

For example, if bitcoin is trading at $50,000 and we think that in a year it will be at $100,000, we might purchase a futures contract at $50,000. If the price falls to $10,000, then we are liable for a $40,000 loss to close out the contract.

If, instead, we choose to trade an options contract, we can limit our downside at the cost of giving up some of the potential upside.

For example, we could go to an options trading venue (such as Deribit) and find an options contract for a year from now with a strike price of $50,000. Suppose, for this example, the premium we would pay to buy this contract is $10,000. We could pay

$10,000 to buy the contract and wait for the contract to expire in a year's time.

If, in a year's time, the price of bitcoin is $100,000, we execute the contract (cash settled) and make a profit of $40,000.

Profit of the contract: $100,000(Settlement price)
- $50,000(Strike price) = $50,000
Premium paid: -$10,000
= $40,000

However, if the price falls to $10,000 at the time of settlement, we simply choose not to execute the contract; our loss is capped at the $10,000 we paid to buy the contract.

With options contracts, your loss is limited but your potential profit is unlimited.

Options can be traded in both directions, with the two option types being 'call' options or 'put' options, both working in the same way but in opposing directions.
The options contract we outlined above is a simple 'call' option contract where the buyer profits if the price of the underlying asset goes up.
However, if you felt that the price of bitcoin might go down, you could buy a 'put' option in a similar way.

For example, if bitcoin is trading at $50,000 and we feel it will crash to $10,000 in a year's time, we could profit from this by purchasing a put option that gives us the option to sell bitcoin in a year's time at the agreed strike price.

If we purchase a put option for a year's time with a strike price of $50,000 and pay a premium of $10,000 and in a years time the price of bitcoin has fallen to $10,000 we make a profit of $30,000

Profit of the contract: $50,000(Strike price) - $10,000 (Settlement price) = $40,000
Premium paid: -$10,000
= $30,000

By purchasing put options, you can limit your potential downside and protect the value of your investment if you are worried it might crash. This could then be seen as buying 'insurance' on your bitcoin in order to protect you from market volatility.

In the above scenario, if we were wrong in our prediction and the price of bitcoin rose to $100,000, we simply do not execute the contract and once again our loss is capped at the premium we paid; in this case the $10,000 premium.

If, instead, we took the other side of options trading, we would be the party selling these options contracts and would collect the premiums immediately but take on the risk of the trade going against us.

Selling options is a popular trade done by traders looking for income replacement, such as retirees, if they hold a lot of the underlying asset. For example, if you held 100 bitcoin and were looking to make some passive income from them, an idea might be to sell what are known as 'covered calls', in which you sell options contracts and collect the premium.

If you held the bitcoin and felt that you would be comfortable selling one if the price hit $100,000, you could sell a call option and take the premium as income. In the event that bitcoin hits $200,000, you're happy as your 100 bitcoin are worth substantially more, but you are effectively forced to sell one of them for $100,000 (the option buyer executes the contract to buy from you for $100,000). However, you received the premium for selling the contract.

In the event that bitcoin doesn't hit $100,000, you pocket the premium and profit from it.

The current price of the underlying asset versus the strike price of the options contract is described as being 'in the money' or 'out of the money', depending on whether it is profitable to the buyer or not. So a call option for $50,000, if bitcoin is at $100,000, is '$50k in the money', but if the price of bitcoin is $40,000, then it is '$10k out of the money'.

The premium for options is agreed between buyers and sellers, and the further the strike price is 'out of the money', the lower the premium that can be demanded for it. This pricing mechanism simply follows the supply and demand principles of any market.

For a seller, the closer the contract is sold 'to the money', the higher the premium you can command, but your risk is obviously higher. In the example of our retiree selling a strike price of $100,000 when bitcoin is at $50,000, that would be considered a 'deep out of the money' contract and would command a lower premium to compensate for its lower risk.

When buying an options contract, you need the price of the underlying asset to move past your strike price by more than the premium you paid in order to profit. An options contract with a strike of $50,000 and a premium of $10,000 would not be profitable for you even if the price of bitcoin hit $59,999, as the profit from the options contract is still less than the premium you paid.

Finally, given the supply and demand dynamics of premium pricing, it is possible to infer potential future price predictions by examining the premium demand for various strike prices at future dates. This indicates where buyers and sellers agree on a premium for a given strike price at a future date, providing insight into where both sides of the market believe the price may be at that time.

10

Institutional Adoption

> *"Institutional adoption of Bitcoin is like watching a herd of elephants tap-dance. There's a lot of weight behind it, but it's going to be awkward and hilarious."*
> *— Unknown*

For as long as I have been involved in Bitcoin, and in fact for longer than that, the annual adage in the bitcoin community has been, 'This is the year that the institutions are coming.'

That was true back as early as 2015, when the first bitcoin-tracking exchange products were listed on the Swedish stock exchange, and the idea has continued to gain new impetus every year as new products and possibilities have been developed. In hindsight, I think that, by most measures, consensus will show that 2024 was the year that bitcoin crossed the institutional chasm. When BlackRock and Fidelity are shepherding hundreds of billions of dollars of bitcoin, and both sides of the US presidential race are openly touting their pro-bitcoin policies, it's hard to come to any conclusion other than that Bitcoin has crossed the political and institutional Rubicon, and the genie has no interest in returning to its bottle.

ETFs

Perhaps the single biggest symbol of institutional adoption of bitcoin has been the approval, finally, of the US spot bitcoin exchange-traded funds. Exchange-Traded Funds, or ETFs for short, were invented in the early 1990s as a means to efficiently trade a basket of underlying investments in a single product.

Prior to that, investors wanting to invest in multiple companies would have to buy individual shares in each company. For example, an investor might purchase 10 shares of Apple stock, 20 shares of Microsoft, etc. This becomes very inefficient and costly if you want to hold a small allocation to many companies, as each one would need an individual transaction, and you may not be able to afford a minimum of one full share in each company.

ETFs solve this by acting as a basket that holds thousands of different investments and lets you purchase a share of that basket. The first ETF ever launched was the SPDR S&P 500 ETF (SPY) on the 22nd January 1993, which purchased a market-cap-weighted share in each of the 500 biggest companies in the United States. The fund itself traded on the stock market and could be bought and sold just like any other stock. Investors who wanted to have investment in all 500 of the top companies in the US could now simply buy shares of this ETF and thereby own a share of the basket that in turn held shares of all of the top 500 companies.

ETFs in and of themselves have been a revolutionary technology for the traditional finance world and arguably one of the single most democratising developments in investing in the last century. Today, ETFs exist for a wide range of things. The largest ETFs still track a basket of global shares, such as VWRD, a global fund from Vanguard that holds over 3,600 stocks from around the world. There are geographically focused ETFs, such as EIDO, which holds shares in 87 Indonesian companies, and thematic ETFs, such as ICLN, which holds shares in 127 clean energy companies. There are also real estate ETFs (known as Real Estate Investment Trusts (REITs)) which hold property and disburse the rental income as dividends, such as iShares IDWP which holds real estate globally. Finally, there are also commodities ETFs, such as GLD, which holds some $62 billion of gold.

The key innovation with ETFs is that they allow the trillions of dollars of retail investment money to easily and readily access these funds in a familiar and regulated manner. Prior to the launch of the gold ETF, anyone seeking to invest in gold would need to broker a deal directly with a gold refiner or seller and then arrange for custody of the gold or take physical delivery of it. This involved risks of fraud and generally resulted in a tricky, cumbersome, and expensive process. At the time of the launch of the gold ETF in November 2004, an ounce of gold sold for $442. By 2010, that price would rise to almost $1,200, almost

275% higher in six years, thanks in no small part to the new accessibility for retail investors to purchase gold reliably and securely via ETFs with a few simple clicks on their computers.

Bitcoin ETFs

The first attempt to establish an ETF for bitcoin started in 2013 when the Gemini exchange founders, Tyler and Cameron Winklevoss, filed for an ETF that would hold bitcoin and issue shares in the fund.

The US Securities and Exchange Commission rejected this proposal, and continued to reject any similar proposals every time they were filed for the next decade.

This hostile policy towards bitcoin ETFs continued through 2021, with all proposals for ETFs being rejected, citing nebulous and unsubstantiated concerns regarding bitcoin market price manipulation, surveillance, or other vaguely worded issues.

Progress towards a bitcoin ETF started in December 2017 when the Chicago Board Options Exchange listed bitcoin futures contracts. The CBOE, in this capacity, is regulated not by the SEC but by the Commodity Futures Trading Commission (CFTC), which in general has been far less hostile towards bitcoin and felt comfortable enough with bitcoin to permit the futures contracts to trade on the licensed and regulated CBOE.

This CBOE listing gave legitimacy to bitcoin via a regulated, government-administered exchange venue on which it traded and laid the ground stone for the next step. With bitcoin futures contracts trading on a regulated exchange, proposals were put forward by ETF issuers to issue an ETF that held and traded the CBOE futures contracts and thereby gave the ETF direct exposure to the price of bitcoin. Since this ETF only held exposure to regulated and approved trading instruments, there could be no real prospect of the ETF being rejected without thereby invalidating the listing of the futures contracts on the CBOE. Either the futures contracts were safe to trade, or they were not, and by 2021 they had been trading for four years and brought in significant volume and revenue to the CBOE and other market participants.

On October 19th 2021, the SEC approved the first ever bitcoin futures ETF, BITO, which began trading on the New York Stock Exchange (NYSE), quickly rising to take in billions of dollars.

However, applications for a pure bitcoin ETF that would simply hold bitcoin directly, also known as a 'spot bitcoin ETF', continued to be rejected by the SEC with increasingly untenable reasons given. By this point, bitcoin futures contracts traded on the CBOE and ETFs tracking the price of bitcoin traded on the NYSE.

A large cryptocurrency investment firm by the name of 'Grayscale' initiated an investment vehicle known as the 'Grayscale Bitcoin Trust' (GBTC) in September of 2013, which acted very similar to a bitcoin ETF but was not permitted to trade like an ETF on the main US exchanges. The structure of the vehicle as a trust also meant it did not need approval from the SEC to operate. The fund had a few differences from an ETF, such as an inability to sell the fund back to the issuer or 'redeem' the funds, and was only available for sale via less liquid 'OTC' trading venues. Nonetheless, the trust acted and operated very much the same as an ETF and grew in size to several billion dollars.

In light of the 2021 bitcoin futures ETF approval, Grayscale filed an application with the SEC to convert this trust into an ETF and sought the approval to do so.

The SEC, in further evidence of their groundless opposition to bitcoin, denied approval for the ETF on June 29, 2022, citing that the proposed ETF would not be 'designed to prevent fraudulent and manipulative acts and practices' without specifying any further details or examples.

Grayscale, however, chose not to take this ruling at face value, given the approvals of the bitcoin futures ETF that would self-evidently prove that this concern must either apply to those too or not at all. Grayscale proceeded to sue the SEC in the US Court of Appeals on the grounds that such a rejection was arbitrary and capricious.

On August 29 2023, the US Court of Appeals ruled in favour of Grayscale and explicitly found that the SEC had indeed acted 'arbitrarily and capriciously' in its denial of the GBTC ETF when considering the previous approval of the bitcoin futures ETFs.

This left the SEC with really only three possible next moves:

1. Approve the ETF
2. Refuse the ETF with new reasoning - which would almost certainly lead to further legal action from Grayscale
3. Refuse the ETF and revoke the bitcoin futures ETFs - which would almost certainly lead to legal action from Grayscale and the bitcoin futures ETF issuers.

In the wake of this, the world's largest investment companies jumped on board and submitted their proposals for bitcoin ETFs. Proposals from BlackRock, Fidelity, and others hit the SEC for approval, and these are large players that simply do not lose. By now bitcoin ETFs existed already in several other countries' stock markets, including over the border in Canada, and the grounds for sustaining a rejection were increasingly untenable.

The deadline for approval or denial for the ARK 21 Shares bitcoin ETF was the 10th January 2024, and would be the final deadline by which the SEC would have to approve or deny the proposal, and the first time it would be forced into such a decision since the US Court of Appeals hearing. The SEC understood that if it gave approval to a spot ETF, it would need to approve all of them at the same time in order to prevent any one fund getting a head start on the market, and so on the 10th January 2024, the SEC voted by three votes to two in favour of approving all of the pending bitcoin spot ETFs. In a clear example of the SEC's arbitrary and capricious hatred of bitcoin, even under ruling from the US Court of Appeals, the SEC still voted two votes to three in favour of rejecting the proposals.

Trading of the ETFs began on the 11th January 2024, and has seen hundreds of billions of dollars traded and the funds growing to hold several hundreds of billions of dollars of assets.

By almost any measure, the ETFs have been the fastest growing and most successful ETF launches in history, by a large margin, and show simply how large the pent-up demand for these regulated ETF products has been for the last decade in which the SEC continued to deny all applications for them.

In the six months since the approval, bitcoin hit new all time highs in US dollar price, and rose over 50% in value. The ease of purchase and the regulated environment have helped millions of retail investors get price exposure to bitcoin, as well as corporate treasuries and pension funds allocating capital to the asset class.

ETNs

Prior to the colossal fight for a bitcoin ETF in the US, other countries already had similar exchange-traded products, such as exchange-traded notes that tracked bitcoin and ether prices on the Swedish stock market.

Launched in May 2015, the Bitcoin Tracker ONE is essentially an unsecured credit note issued by the company XBT Provider AB (Publ), which entitles the bearer to the financial value of a fixed number of bitcoin. In structuring the product this way, it avoided some of the more onerous regulation on ETF issuance but also introduced credit risk, as the note does not legally grant ownership of the underlying asset and is, in fact, just an unsecured credit note.

Nonetheless, the ETNs tracked broadly in line with the price of bitcoin and provided traditional finance investors access to bitcoin's price exposure, provided that they had access to the Swedish Nasdaq (which most brokerages do).
The note trades in euros and Swedish krona, and was the vehicle through which I personally first got exposure to bitcoin as an investment asset.

Moreover, in 2018, a new investment company was launched called '21Shares' (the same 21Shares that launched a bitcoin ETF in the US). 21Shares has since gone on to list almost 40 exchange-traded products, including various cryptocurrencies such as BNB (Binance Coin) and others, as well as baskets of coins wrapped under a single ETP, leveraged ETPs, and even inverse ETPs.

Whilst not technically ETNs, these funds do appear to also not be full ETFs and sit somewhere in between the two as simply 'exchange-traded products', which, from my reading of the investor disclosures, seem to enjoy more credibility than ETNs and avoid the unsecured credit note risk. However, they are not as widely available to retail investors as an ETF. Nonetheless, it could easily be argued that 21Shares in Switzerland is leading the market here and showing what the potential future ETF landscape in the US will look like in a few years.

Corporate Holdings

Whilst the ETF issuance now makes it substantially easier for corporations and investment funds to allocate money to bitcoin, there has been a slew of corporations that have decided to put bitcoin on their corporate balance sheets and hold it as a core part of their corporate treasury.

MicroStrategy

By far the most well-known company to add bitcoin to its balance sheet has to be MicroStrategy, led by its enigmatic leader Michael Saylor.

MicroStrategy is a business intelligence software development company, located in Virginia, United States. The company was founded in 1989 by Michael Saylor, who remains the executive chairman today. Saylor retains a substantial double-digit equity stake in the company and a significant voice on the board of directors, which allows him to be more decisive and nimble with the company's direction and governance.

By mid 2020, the company had accumulated cash reserves in the region of $500 million and sought to put this money to use somewhere. In subsequent interviews, Saylor described the $500 million on the balance sheet as like a large block of ice that the company was sitting on, slowly melting as inflation chips away at the purchasing power of the money. Seeking some safe haven to shield the purchasing power of the company balance sheet, and during the forced lockdowns of the COVID-

19 pandemic, Saylor discovered bitcoin and began to lay the groundwork for converting MicroStrategy to a bitcoin-centric company built around a corporate treasury denominated in bitcoin.

In August 2020, MicroStrategy became the first major publicly traded company to openly announce they intended to purchase bitcoin to hold on the corporate balance sheet. The company announced that they would deploy the $500 million in company holdings in two tranches. Firstly, they would commit $250 million to buy stock back from the open market at the prevailing market rate. This is a typical endeavour of publicly listed companies in order to increase the share price by removing shares from circulation, thereby driving up the share price as the same company is now split among fewer shares. In this case, Saylor announced the $250 million share buyback as a compromise with the board in order to provide a liquidity event for shareholders to sell their shares back to the company in case they did not agree with the more radical second tranche of the plan: buying $250 million of bitcoin.

On the 11th August 2020, MicroStrategy announced they had purchased 21,454 bitcoin at an aggregate cost of $250 million.

In subsequent months, the company has continued to purchase bitcoin using the free cash flow generated by the business, as well as through substantial bond offerings that have raised external capital:

December 2020: $650 million in convertible senior notes.
February 2021: $1.05 billion in convertible senior notes.
June 2021: $500 million in senior secured notes.

March 2024: $800 million in convertible senior notes
March 2024: $603.8 million in convertible senior notes
June 2024: $800 million in convertible senior notes

As of October 2024 the company has acquired 252,220 bitcoin, over 1% of the entire number of bitcoin that will ever exist. The bitcoin are currently valued around $15.3 billion and were purchased at an aggregate cost of around $9.91 billion.

MicroStrategy as a bitcoin ETF

Given the heel-dragging that occurred with the bitcoin ETF approval in the US, MicroStrategy embracing bitcoin as their reserve asset positioned the company as a regulated vehicle by which investors could get exposure to bitcoin. As the company aggressively ramped up its ownership of bitcoin, the value of the company became increasingly driven by its reserve asset holdings, and as a result, the share price of MicroStrategy began to trade quite closely in lockstep with the price of bitcoin. In the period before January 2024, with no ETF yet approved, MicroStrategy began to see substantial inflows into their shares from investors seeking bitcoin exposure, which led to the share price trading at a substantial premium above the book value of the assets held and the business.

If the business may be fairly valued at, for example, $5 billion, and the value of all the assets the company holds (including bitcoin) is another $5 billion, then the company should trade at a $10 billion valuation. If there were then a billion shares in circulation, the fair market value of the shares would be

$10. However, the overwhelming demand for shares may drive the share price up to, for example, $12, which would give the company a $12 billion valuation or a premium of $2 billion above what the company should be reasonably valued at.

As the demand for regulated bitcoin access was unmet by a spot bitcoin ETF, the flows into MicroStrategy stock did, indeed, drive the price of shares to a premium which the company was able to capitalise on by issuing and selling new shares to dilute the existing shareholders of the premium and raise money for the company. In Q4 of 2023, the company issued 2,266,503 new shares and raised $1.2 billion that it used to purchase more bitcoin.

The approach taken by MicroStrategy here has frequently been referred to as a 'speculative attack' on the US dollar by borrowing dollars in substantial size and then converting them to bitcoin. Given the long date of the bonds issued, their convertibility for shares, the low interest rates on the bonds, and the fact that the company continues to generate free cash flow from its main business, the company seems well placed to meet its obligations on the bonds and its repayments without having cause to sell the bitcoin it holds on its books. The company has no intention to sell any of its bitcoin and continues to aggressively acquire more. The lack of an ETF and the fact that the company moved first in this area gave MicroStrategy an advantage that would no longer be replicable for others. However, each company that were to replicate this bitcoin acquisition strategy would be better placed than any company that did it after them, given the scarce nature of bitcoin.

Tesla

At the time of writing, the only other well-known publicly-listed US company that has added bitcoin to its corporate balance sheet is the electric vehicle manufacturer, Tesla.

Led by the enigmatic and eccentric CEO, Elon Musk, Tesla announced on the 8th February 2021 that the company had invested $1.5 billion of its corporate treasury in bitcoin, acquiring a total of 43,200 bitcoin, and that the company would begin accepting bitcoin as a payment method for its electric vehicles. The news led to a rapid increase in the price of bitcoin of around 19%, jumping from approximately $38,800 up to $46,300.

The company's foray into bitcoin, however, would soon prove to be fairly short-lived, as they announced in April of the same year that the company had sold 10% of its bitcoin (4,320 bitcoin), ostensibly to 'test the liquidity of the market'. This was followed shortly afterwards, in May, with the announcement that they would no longer be accepting bitcoin as a method of payment.

In the earnings report of Q2 2022, Tesla further announced that it had sold 75% of its remaining bitcoin, leaving a net balance of 9,720 bitcoin, which remains on the corporate treasury.

Tesla has shown no intention to purchase or sell bitcoin from its treasury in the previous two years, nor any intention to integrate bitcoin as a method of payment.

Tether

Another prominent company, albeit a non-public one, that holds a substantial bitcoin position on its corporate treasury is Tether, the issuer of the USDT stablecoin.

At the time of writing, there were over 112 billion USDT tokens in circulation, which the company backs primarily with US dollar-denominated US Treasury bills and other short- and long-term US dollar-denominated debt instruments. However, in May 2023, the company revealed that a small percentage of the company's treasury continues to be allocated to both bitcoin and gold.

In the same announcement, the company also revealed a forward guidance that it would take up to 15% of corporate profits each quarter and commit to converting that into bitcoin to increase the number of bitcoin held on its balance sheet.

As of the most recent update from April 2024, Tether purchased an additional 8,888 bitcoin in Q1 of 2024, bringing its total to 75,354 bitcoin worth in the region of $5 billion and making it the holder of the seventh-largest single bitcoin wallet address.

Others

Aside from the large headline-grabbing companies that hold bitcoin on their corporate balance sheets, there are also many other public companies that also hold bitcoin, including Coinbase (9,480 bitcoin), Marathon Digital Holdings (17,857 bitcoin),

Block Inc (8,038 bitcoin), and many more.

Moreover, there are hundreds, if not thousands, of private companies that hold bitcoin on their balance sheets, though data on those are obviously much harder to find. Some private companies have, however, been quite open about their bitcoin holdings, such as the Tahini's restaurant chain in Canada that converts all of its cash reserves into bitcoin and has since mid-2020.

Other private companies that openly operate on a 'bitcoin standard' include the famous Bitcoin podcast 'What Bitcoin Did' and its sister company 'Real Bedford FC', both run by Bitcoiner and podcaster Peter McCormack.

Nation States

Throughout the history of Bitcoin, nation states have tangentially interacted with the network and the underlying bitcoin transacted across it. In many cases, nation states have seized bitcoin as part of criminal investigations and often later auctioned it off. In very few cases, we have seen nation states or senior members of the governing apparatus of the state positively embrace bitcoin.

El Salvador

By far and away, the nation-state that has most fully embraced Bitcoin would be the small Latin American country of El Salvador.

Lying to the south of Guatemala and west of Honduras in Central America, the little country of El Salvador is home to 6.5 million people and led by the charismatic millennial President Nayib Bukele. Historically, the nation has faced significant issues with organised crime and gang violence, as well as decades of domestic corruption. The economy of the country remains heavily dependent on remittances from overseas, primarily from the United States and other countries in the region.

Following years of domestic economic and social problems, the country officially dropped support for its own native currency in favour of the US dollar on the 1st January 2001. This 'dollarisation' of the economy helped stem domestic inflation and encourage external investment, but also sowed the seeds of adoption of an external currency, and eased the flow of funds into the country from overseas by removing currency conversion with the domestic currency.

After coming to power in 2019, President Bukele embarked on a strong and radical campaign of sweeping domestic reform across the country, eradicating corruption and taking on the criminal gangs in the country head-on. Despite early condemnation from some NGOs and human rights organisations, the reforms have been massively popular within the country, with the homicide rate per 100,000 people collapsing from the highest in the world at 38.8 in 2019 to 2.0 in 2024.

Buoyed by the broad support for his sweeping reforms, in June 2021, live on stage at the Bitcoin2021 conference in Miami, President Bukele announced his intent to bring a bill before the legislative assembly in El Salvador to make bitcoin legal tender in the country.

The bill passed a few days later on the 9th of June, with broad support, and came into effect on the 7th September of the same year, making El Salvador the first country globally to make bitcoin legal tender and marking another important milestone in the history of Bitcoin.

The legal tender law mandates that bitcoin must be accepted within the country as a means of settlement for purchases and debts. To facilitate this, the government launched their own bitcoin wallet that had Lightning Network support as well as mainchain Bitcoin. This was incentivised by providing $30 of bitcoin to each citizen that downloaded and set up the government wallet app known as ‘Chivo’ (a Salvadoran slang word for ‘cool’). Overnight, local stores, including multinational chains such as McDonald’s, Starbucks, and others, began accepting bitcoin for purchases and continue to do so to this day.

In addition to making bitcoin legal tender, the government of El Salvador became the first country to directly purchase bitcoin to place as an asset in the country’s national reserve. Despite the fluctuations of the price of bitcoin over the previous three years leading to the value of the bitcoin purchases being deeply in the red at times—and the government being widely criticised by foreign journalists—at the time of writing, the government of El Salvador holds some 5,779 bitcoin and is comfortably in profit in excess of 50%.

In January 2022, the International Monetary Fund (IMF) sharply criticised the Salvadoran government for its embrace of bitcoin and threatened to withhold $1.3 billion in development loans unless the country reversed the law. El Salvador refused to repeal the law and continued to buy more bitcoin throughout the market downturn of 2021-2022.

Whilst the impact on the remittances economy within the country is unclear, one of the runaway successes of the implementation of bitcoin and related policies has been a substantial boon in the tourism sector within the country. As of early 2023, President Bukele announced that tourism into El Salvador had grown by 95%, with the vast majority of that being from bitcoin holders and enthusiasts visiting or relocating to the country. At the time of writing, it remains possible to gain permanent residency in El Salvador for an investment of three bitcoin into the country, or to obtain Salvadoran citizenship with a donation of $1 million USD in bitcoin or USDT to the government.

Other Countries

Whilst no other countries have gone as far as El Salvador in the adoption of bitcoin, there are several nations that have some involvement with Bitcoin in various ways.

Central African Republic

The Central African Republic (CAR) became the second country to adopt bitcoin as legal tender on the 27th April 2022. However, this was rather comically overturned nine days later, in an extraordinary general meeting on the 6th May of the same year, during which the law was repealed and the use of cryptocurrency in the country was banned.

Bhutan

The small Buddhist kingdom of Bhutan is a remote country nestled on the eastern edge of the Himalayan mountain range. By all accounts, it is far from a hub of finance or technology, but the secretive kingdom, under the guidance of its monarch Jigme Khesar Namgyel Wangchuck, also known as the 'Dragon King', has been engaged in bitcoin mining using the country's abundant hydropower reserves since at least 2019.

Whilst the secretive and reclusive nature of the country makes ascertaining concrete details difficult, Forbes reported in 2023 that the kingdom held exposure to the collapsed cryptocurrency platforms Celsius and FTX, which led to the government of Bhutan acknowledging its involvement in mining and holding of bitcoin via its sovereign wealth fund, Druk Holdings & Investment (DHI).

Whilst the scale and size of Bhutan's bitcoin mining efforts remain unknown, it is understood that the nation has been mining bitcoin since bitcoin was priced around $5,000 per coin and has amassed several hundreds of millions of dollars of bitcoin on the nation's books.

Tonga

In the days and weeks following the announcement that El Salvador was to adopt bitcoin as legal tender in the country, some other countries that were in similar economic circumstances began to look at the idea with interest. One country that took some steps towards this is the Polynesian kingdom of Tonga.

An archipelago of some 170 islands in the South Pacific, the country has a population of around 100,000 and a GDP of less than $500 million USD.

In late 2021, a Tongan politician and 'Noble of the Realm', Lord Fusitu'a, came to prominence globally in the Bitcoin community for his advocacy of the currency and his intention to table a bill before the domestic parliament for the adoption of bitcoin as legal tender in the country.

Lord Fusitu'a was a larger-than-life and very affable character with whom I had the chance to interact on several occasions.

Sadly, he vacated his seat before the November 2021 Tongan elections due to seeking medical care outside of the country and being unable to campaign.

Lord Fusitu'a passed away in February 2024, and Tonga currently has no plans to adopt bitcoin as legal tender.

Virunga National Park

One of the more interesting quasi-governmental adoptions of bitcoin in recent years has been the integration of bitcoin mining equipment powered by hydropower within the Virunga National Park in the Democratic Republic of Congo.

The national park, situated in the war-torn and often lawless region of the Democratic Republic of Congo, spans over 8,000 kilometres and is home to an array of endangered animals, including mountain gorillas, various mammals, and reptiles.

Given the nature of the region and the difficulties faced in administering the park by the central government, the park receives only a fraction of the funding required for its maintenance from the government in Kinshasa.

In early 2023, it was widely reported that the park had turned to tapping into its natural hydropower reserves to power extensive bitcoin mining operations since as early as 2020. With rebel kidnappings in 2018, Ebola in 2019, and COVID in 2020 effectively closing the park for tourism, it was unable to generate any revenue for its maintenance. Reports from early 2023 claimed that the park was running bitcoin mining operations and hoped to earn as much as $150,000 per month from these, which would be used to pay salaries and the upkeep of the park.

11

Hacks & Fraud

> *"Amateurs hack systems; professionals hack people."*
> *— Bruce Schneier*

The majority of Bitcoin hacks happen at the personal level. As we covered in earlier chapters, ownership of the private key that controls your bitcoin is the ownership of your bitcoin, and losing or sharing that private key gives anyone who knows it the ability to steal your bitcoin.

At the personal level, most hacks involve social manipulation to trick a user into giving up their private key or their 12-word seed phrase, or hacking into systems where a user has stored that private key or seed phrase—such as compromising an Apple Cloud account or other online storage system where a user may have stored their key or phrase.

For this reason, it is advisable to never store your seed phrase on a digital device and instead record it offline, either with a trusty pen and paper or by etching it into steel plates. Etching your seed phrase into steel plates gives the benefit of it surviving exposure to fire or flood.

Other personal hacks include hijacking users' software in order to route payments to addresses other than those intended. These include exploiting known vulnerabilities in older Bitcoin wallet software—which is why you should always update your wallet software to the latest stable version. In other cases, hackers hijack the clipboard on your device to swap a destination Bitcoin address that you copied and intended to send to with a wallet address owned by the malicious actor.

From a security point of view, it is almost always preferable to store your bitcoin in an offline cold wallet that is not connected to the internet. Whilst this has the downside of making sending your bitcoin less convenient, it also greatly reduces the risk of a bad actor being able to extract your private key and steal your bitcoin.

Thankfully, as Bitcoin has developed over the years, products and software have been developed to mitigate the risk of these hacks. If you are holding any meaningful quantity of bitcoin today, then storing it on a dedicated hardware wallet is a good step to mitigate the risk from hackers. These hardware wallets store the private key securely on the Hardware Security Module (HSM) of the device and never transmit it off the device to any other computer. Using a dedicated hardware device and storing your seed phrase securely—etched into steel plates—is the best practice for most users.

If you hold or intend to hold a substantial quantity of bitcoin, it is advisable to use a multi-sig solution that requires signing with several keys—each held on dedicated hardware wallets that are geographically separate. This adds additional protection against in-person attacks where a malicious actor breaks into your home and subjects you to violence in order to steal your bitcoin. With a multi-sig wallet using several keys stored on hardware devices that are held in separate locations, it is not possible to send bitcoin without visiting the physical location of your hardware wallet keys. Placing them in separate locations, such as your office or a bank vault, would render it impossible for an attacker to sustain violence or the threat of violence against you through multiple public and high-security locations without an alarm being raised.

If you use wrapped bitcoin on another chain and interact with Decentralised Finance (DeFi) protocols, there comes another level of risk with the permissions granted on that chain. For example, if you authorise a DeFi protocol the ability to manage your wrapped bitcoin, that permission could be hijacked to steal your bitcoin. In general, when using wrapped bitcoin on other chains, there is no specific advice other than to remain vigilant and exercise extreme caution in all of your interactions on that chain.

Exchanges

The majority of hacks that make headlines are not attacks on a personal level, but exploits of protocols that are widely used in the non-Bitcoin crypto industry, or hacks on exchanges where many customers' funds are held. The centralised nature of exchanges makes them a prime target, given they hold so much bitcoin at a single point of failure.

Mt.Gox

Perhaps the most infamous exchange hack in Bitcoin's history is the one that occurred on the Mt. Gox exchange, culminating in the collapse of the exchange in February 2014. To date, the hack remains the single largest in terms of the number of bitcoin stolen.

From 2011 to its collapse in 2014, Mt. Gox became the single largest Bitcoin trading platform. It had initially been built as a platform for buying and trading Magic: The Gathering playing cards (hence the name Mt. Gox—Magic: The Gathering Online Exchange). The exchange began offering bitcoin trading in July of 2010, before it was sold in March of 2011 to Mark Karpelès, a French software engineer who lived in Tokyo and went by the online alias MagicalTux.

Beginning sometime in 2011, issues with the way the exchange processed bitcoin withdrawals were exploited by hackers to withdraw significantly more bitcoin than they had available in their accounts, using an attack known as a 'malleability exploit'. Between a certain point in 2011 and the eventual collapse of the exchange in February 2014, unknown hackers were able to withdraw bitcoin from their accounts to external wallets and then trick the internal system of Mt. Gox into thinking the withdrawal had not occurred, allowing them to make further withdrawals of the bitcoin they had already withdrawn.

Over the space of three weeks, the largest bitcoin exchange in the world at the time came to a complete halt, and some 850,000 bitcoin were revealed to have been stolen; worth some $450 million at the time, the coins today would be valued at almost $52 billion.

February 7, 2014: Mt. Gox halted all bitcoin withdrawals, citing technical issues related to transaction malleability. This led to growing customer complaints and concerns about the financial status of the exchange.
February 17, 2014: With withdrawals still halted, Mt. Gox's situation worsened, impacting bitcoin's value negatively.
February 20, 2014: Mt. Gox's bitcoin prices dropped to below 20% of those on other exchanges due to growing market concerns.
February 24, 2014: Mt. Gox suspended all trading and its website went offline. An alleged leaked internal document claimed that the company was insolvent after losing 744,408 bitcoin to theft.
February 28, 2014: Mt. Gox filed for bankruptcy protection in Japan.

In the days and weeks that followed, the price of bitcoin fell some 36%, and users began legal proceedings against Karpelès in Tokyo.

Karpelès was initially arrested in August of 2015 on charges of embezzlement and false accounting. In March of 2019, he was eventually found not guilty of embezzlement but guilty of false accounting to cover up the losses at the exchange, and was sentenced to 30 months' imprisonment, suspended for four years—sparing him from jail.

Prosecutors and investors were ultimately able to recover some 130,000 bitcoin, and legal proceedings have been prolonged regarding the process of returning them to affected users.

As of July 2024, a decade later, 41.5% of the recovered bitcoin has been distributed to affected creditors.

Bitfinex

One of the most significant hacks in Bitcoin history was the attack on Bitfinex that occurred on the 2nd of August 2016. Hackers were able to gain unauthorised access to Bitfinex's system and exploit a weakness in the setup and execution of the multi-sig wallets that the exchange used to process client withdrawals. The hackers were able to withdraw 119,756 bitcoin, worth $72 million at the time.
The market reacted to the news of the theft with an almost immediate sell-off, seeing bitcoin's price collapse from around $605 to $515, taking around 20% off the price.

In response, Bitfinex immediately halted all trading, deposits, and withdrawals on their platform, before announcing that the exchange would socialise losses across all account holders, with all users seeing their deposits 'haircut' by 36.067%, regardless of whether their accounts had been directly affected by the hack. However, all users would be credited with a corresponding amount of a newly issued token, BFX. The exchange would buy back these tokens from the market over time using its profits to compensate victims, or the tokens could be traded in for equity in the parent company behind the exchange. By April 2017, the exchange had bought back all of the outstanding BFX tokens, and users had been fully compensated for their loss. Those who had converted the tokens for equity in the company have since seen significant returns over and above their initial loss amount.

No progress was made on finding the culprits of the attack for many years until February 2022, when the US authorities announced the arrest of Ilya Lichtenstein and his wife Heather R. Morgan in New York.

The unlikely hacker couple, in their early thirties, were accused of having been behind the hack. Both pleaded guilty and are awaiting sentencing at the time of writing. The attention that the high-profile arrests brought led to Heather becoming an overnight internet celebrity as people dug up rap videos she had made under the stage name 'Razzlekhan' on YouTube.

They are, however, unrelated to Bitcoin, and fucking cringe.

Binance

Thankfully, over time, hacks against exchanges have decreased in both size and the number of bitcoin stolen. A more recent large-scale hack occurred on the 7th May 2019, at the exchange Binance, with hackers stealing 7,074 bitcoin valued at approximately $40 million at the time.

At the time of this attack, I was working at Binance and recall the incident in detail. I woke up on the morning of the 8th and checked Twitter to see a rumour circulating regarding an unusual bitcoin withdrawal from a known Binance wallet address. The withdrawal of over 7,000 bitcoin in a single transaction from the known Binance 'hot wallet' was unusual, and due to the public nature of the blockchain, this was immediately detected by anyone monitoring the network. Two main theories were forming: either this was a hack and someone had stolen the bitcoin, or Binance had accidentally sent the large sum incorrectly while rotating funds between internal wallets.

Seeing in the internal chat groups that the public relations team were silent and had been pulled into newly spun up chat groups to immediately war plan the public response to the incident, it was immediately clear to me that something was quite wrong here and this was not just a wild goose chase whipped up by social media.

Shortly thereafter, the press team released a statement on the Binance website confirming that there had been a security breach of the Binance systems resulting in the theft of over 7,074 bitcoin. They announced that deposits and withdrawals were indefinitely suspended and that Binance would cover 100% of the losses from its own funds.

The CEO of Binance, Changpeng Zhao, was scheduled to give a live interview on Twitter and accept questions that very same morning. The interview still went ahead and was instrumental in calming the market. Overall, the hack had minimal impact on the market.

The attack was sophisticated and persistent. In my opinion, it may have been executed by a state actor. It involved compromising multiple machines and remaining dormant inside the IT network of Binance for some time, gaining enhanced access before executing the attack at the most opportune moment in a coordinated attack on multiple systems.

A key part of the attack was compromising a large number of API keys used by clients to withdraw funds. I was in the office next to the API team and recall senior managers urgently communicating in Chinese to disable and revoke all API keys in the hours following the hack.As the dust settled on the attack, I took some time during the day to write down my thoughts on what had contributed to it. I came to two conclusions that were the root causes of problems within the company's security culture that had led to the attack.

The company was still acting like a startup, despite being worth hundreds of billions of dollars.
There was an inherited Asian system of hierarchy that prevented a subordinate questioning a superior.
The first issue was continuing to think like a small startup in terms of making financial savings, which impacted overall security. For the first 18 months of working there, I had to bring my own (untested, unchecked) laptop to work and access work systems. This saved the cost of purchasing a laptop for every employee, but at the cost of having untested devices on sensitive network systems.

The second was an Asian cultural system of not holding a superior to account—for example, if an employee observed a manager cutting corners to save time or money on something that might pose a security risk.

I took both of these findings to Changpeng Zhao (CZ) himself in a one-on-one meeting that very afternoon. He agreed and thanked me for the feedback. By late afternoon, CZ sent an email to the entire company with my observations and suggestions and thanking me by name.

We implemented a strong overhaul of security within the company, excluding all personal devices from any network systems. We also implemented a strict 'If you see something, say something' doctrine that prevented any disciplinary action against employees for reporting security issues caused by anyone, including superiors.

This was thankfully taken very seriously and implemented swiftly by the company. I continued to advocate for best practices internally, even if it did piss off quite a few of my colleagues at the time. Among the work I did with Binance, I think my contribution to overhauling the internal security was one of the most important things I was able to achieve.

Block Re-org

In the immediate aftermath of the hack being announced, some prominent Bitcoin experts floated the idea on social media of performing a 'block re-org' in order to recover the stolen funds.

This was very controversial.

A block re-org would involve getting a majority of the Bitcoin mining power to stop mining on the current chain and revert to the previous chain state before the hacked coins were moved. There, they would re-mine the block, excluding the transfer of the stolen funds, and then continue to mine subsequent blocks, effectively continuing the blockchain with that one transaction excluded.

The biggest hurdle to this was time, as each new block that was mined meant that this re-org would require going back even further. The other hurdle was financial. Each block that was mined provided a reward of 12.5 bitcoin, and miners would expect to be compensated for this, as they had expended energy to mine the blocks that would now be invalidated.

Finally, anyone that had made a transaction on the Bitcoin blockchain since the hack would have their transactions reversed, which could cause significant problems for thousands of exchanges and other systems.

Ultimately, though, this would fundamentally undermine the system of Bitcoin by violating the principle that transactions are final once included in a block. This is a core tenet of Bitcoin and violating it in order to reverse this transaction would show that it could be violated to reverse *any* transaction if the party affected has enough money and social clout.

Despite announcing on the Twitter interview that Binance was 'considering' the block re-org, following internal debate, this idea was not pursued.

Fraud

In addition to hacks, many bitcoin have also been lost to simple fraud. Once again, the largest instances of fraud have been at the personal level, but the largest-scale frauds have occurred on exchanges, given their ability to attract substantial sums of Bitcoin from mass-market retail users.

Personal-level fraud involving Bitcoin can occur in many ways. For example, a person could be scammed into buying bitcoin from another, but then receive testnet bitcoins (which have no value), or some token issued on another chain that is simply named 'bitcoin'. There are also other, more famous, frauds involving Bitcoin such as the July 2020 hack of Twitter.

On the 15th July 2020, Graham Ivan Clark and three accomplices were able to socially engineer several employees at Twitter into giving up their administrative credentials. Using these, the group logged into the administrative system at Twitter to send tweets from 130 high-profile accounts, including those of Joe Biden and Barack Obama, and companies such as Coinbase and Apple.

The tweets were a very low sophistication fraud that simply said that the account holder would double any bitcoin you sent to a specific address.

Given that the accounts were verified on Twitter and the tweets appeared to be genuinely from those accounts, the fraud raised over 12 bitcoin, worth around $120,000 at the time.

As the fraud played out publicly in real-time, I immediately had the team at Binance blacklist the fraudulent address to prevent users from withdrawing to it. Sometimes, proactive measures are necessary to protect users from themselves.

The fraud was a very unsophisticated hack, and the perpetrators were quickly identified and arrested.

Bitconnect

Though there are thousands of scams where users have exchanged bitcoin for cryptocurrencies on other blockchains that promised better returns, one of the most famous is certainly Bitconnect.

Bitconnect encouraged investors to swap bitcoin for their own Bitconnect token, which they would then lend back to the company to use as capital in its automated trading program, sharing in the profits.

The company claimed that an automated trading bot would benefit from Bitcoin price volatility and offered returns as high as 40% per month. The problem, however, was that there was no trading bot, and the operation was simply a Ponzi scheme.

The scheme became popular in late 2017 when an investor was filmed promoting it enthusiastically on stage in Pattaya, Thailand, exclaiming 'Bitconnect!' into a microphone.

The project collapsed in January 2018, leading to a complete loss for most investors. The exact total of the fraud is unclear, but prosecutors alleged it to be between $2.4–3.5 billion.

The founder of the scam, Indian national, Satish Kumbhani, is sought by US and Indian prosecutors and has since disappeared. He is believed to be hiding in India under a false identity.

OneCoin

In a very similar scheme, a company operating from Bulgaria via offshore entities in Dubai, Belize, and other jurisdictions launched OneCoin in 2014. Headed by Ruja Ignatova, the group offered high returns to users for depositing their bitcoin into the system and issued them OneCoin tokens in return.

The OneCoin tokens were never a cryptocurrency and could not be transferred outside of the OneCoin exchange. The company ostensibly sold online training courses as well as their own token, and claimed to give investors a share in cryptocurrency mining operations in Bulgaria and Hong Kong.

In reality, the entire operation was simply a Ponzi scheme that paid out old investors with the deposits of new investors, thereby creating the illusion of success and drawing in additional investors.

The scheme attracted attention from law enforcement around the world, as authorities in Thailand, Belize, Germany, and several EU countries issued warnings about the company in 2017. Ignatova disappeared and has not been seen since.

Prosecutions continued in multiple jurisdictions, with US authorities estimating total investor losses to be in excess of $4 billion.

QuadrigaCX

Of the more prominent exchanges that engaged in fraud, QuadrigaCX is also one of the more interesting fraud cases. Founded in 2013 in Canada by Gerald Cotton, the exchange grew quickly in Canada and took in hundreds of millions of dollars.

In December 2018, Cotten was travelling in India when he was suddenly, and without warning, reported dead by his wife. The cause of death was reported as complications from Crohn's disease. As the sole holder of the keys for the bitcoin and cryptocurrency on the exchange, Cotten's death and subsequent inaccessibility to his encrypted laptop put those funds out of reach. The total amount lost was estimated to be in the region of $250 million Canadian dollars, which was around $190 million USD at the time.

Subsequent investigations suggested that the entire operation was fraudulent and that the funds deposited to the exchange had been intentionally diverted and misappropriated. This theory was heightened by suggestions that obtaining a forged death certificate in India was trivially easy.

Allegations of fraud were further heightened in February 2019 when it was revealed that the cofounder of the exchange was Omar Dhanani, a convicted fraudster that had changed his name to hide his criminal record and was working under the name Michael Patryn.

In June 2020, the Ontario Securities Commission formally declared that the exchange had been operating as a fraud and perpetuating a Ponzi scheme.

FTX, Luna, Three Arrows, Celsius

By quite some margin, the biggest and most spectacular criminal fraud perpetrated in the Bitcoin and cryptocurrency space so far has to be the case of FTX. The exchange was founded in the summer of 2019 and quickly and aggressively grew market share. I opened an account with FTX in the summer of 2019 in order to trade the tokens they had related to the upcoming 2020 US Presidential election. The exchange was pushing the boundaries on the items it allowed users to trade, including markets that acted as proxies for predictions on real world outcomes.

The exchange was technically superior to anything available at the time, seamlessly blending both spot and derivatives markets. It automatically allowed users to leverage their spot holdings as collateral to margin trade derivatives products.

As the nascent exchange grew rapidly and took market share from Binance, it continued to raise investment in the company, including a substantial investment from Binance itself in December 2019.

FTX continued to court controversy through 2020 when its

trading desk was directly accused by the CEO of Binance of attempting to manipulate the Bitcoin futures market on their platform. This accusation stemmed from large and structured orders made via API, causing the price on the Binance platform to disconnect wildly from the market price for a short time and causing issues for users. When called out on this publicly, the CEO of FTX, Sam Bankman-Fried (SBF), admitted to having made the trades but denied any intent to cause the resulting price dislocation, or reputational damage for Binance.

As time drew on, the two CEOs grew increasingly distrustful and even openly resentful of each other, and the relationship soured significantly. SBF pushed aggressively with attempts to gain regulatory approval in the US and spent extensively on marketing, including acquiring the naming rights to the Miami Heat stadium, endorsements from Tom Brady, and a host of other celebrities. SBF even courted political support extensively, appearing on stage with the former US President Bill Clinton and former UK Prime Minister Tony Blair.

At the same time, Binance was facing increasing political headwinds in multiple jurisdictions, but especially the US. In early summer of 2022, the cryptocurrency project Luna began to run into difficulties. The project had been offering 20% yield on USD via their cryptocurrency, and had ballooned to several billion dollars in value. Regrettably, I had missed out on most of this as I had been travelling across Indonesia on a motorbike, but finally decided to get involved and allocated $30,000 to TerraUSD (UST), the USD stablecoin of their system.

A few weeks before, a friend of mine, Algod, had openly bet $1 million against the founder of Luna that the whole scheme was a Ponzi scam that would collapse within a year.

The following weeks were full of bellicose rhetoric on social media as both sides swelled and the project took in billions more dollars each week.

The first sign I got that something was wrong was repeated notifications on my Apple Watch from the FTX exchange that the price of the TerraUSD (UST) stablecoin was significantly de-pegging from the $1 mark. As I rode my motorbike across central Java for four hours, the notifications continued to roll in. By the time I stopped for dinner, the system had effectively collapsed, and the $30,000 I had deposited was essentially lost during the course of my ride.

This spectacular collapse was, ultimately fraud in and of itself and the founder of Luna, Do Kwon ultimately ended up on the run from law enforcement for months, before being found in Montenegro, attempting to board a flight to Dubai using a fake Costa Rican passport. He remains in custody facing extradition to both the US and Korea and several decades in prison.

However, the collapse also sparked a huge wave of contagion in the cryptocurrency markets, which in short order led to the collapse of the Singapore-based hedge fund Three Arrows Capital (3AC). The hedge fund had been on the wrong side of the Luna collapse and imploded, losing billions of dollars of investors' funds, including several bitcoin belonging to friends of mine here in Singapore. At the time of writing, one of the founders of 3AC, Kyle Davies, is reported to be uncontactable, while the other, Su Zhu, has spent time in Singapore's Changi prison.

As the rumours of 3AC collapse trickled out on social media, my friend and long-time Bitcoiner (and author) Anthony Lewis called me and we discussed the latest developments. As I sat on the roadside of Club Street in Singapore, we joked but had no idea of the scale of things that were about to unfold.

The founders of Three Arrows Capital alleged that SBF and the trading arm of FTX orchestrated and abetted the collapse of the Luna system to bankrupt them and remove them from the market. Whether that is true or not, the collapse of the Luna cryptocurrency certainly started a sequence of events that ended with the collapse of FTX itself.

The collapse of Luna led to the collapse of Three Arrows Capital. Their collapse deepened the contagion in the market. It would later be revealed that many large cryptocurrency firms had deep exposure to either Luna or 3AC, having taken client funds and deposited them with those now-defunct companies. This reached as far as Gemini, the exchange I had worked for, which was headed by the Winklevoss twins. Gemini strove to be fully regulated, but allowed clients to earn a yield on their cryptocurrency funds by putting them into a company called Genesis, who ultimately lent those funds to 3AC. The collapse of 3AC meant that Gemini customer funds were now inaccessible.

This further deepened the contagion in the market, leading more companies to fail and prices to collapse, which ultimately significantly impacted trades made by Alameda Research, the sister trading firm of FTX.

As the crisis continued, Alameda was taking substantial losses on the trades it had made in the market, exceeding the funds available to cover these losses.

Fighting for their life and to avoid their own bankruptcy, Alameda ultimately, secretly, tapped into the FTX users' massive client deposits to cover their trading losses and hope that as the market recovered that they would be able to ride out the market crisis. It is alleged that FTX client funds in the region of $10 billion were moved to Alameda to cover the hole in its balance sheet.

Outwardly, there was no sign of distress at FTX or Alameda, and as late as the 26th September 2022, SBF announced that FTX had agreed to a deal with another severely crisis-hit cryptocurrency broker, Voyager Digital, to purchase the distressed company for $1.4 billion.

The final days for FTX started on the 2nd November 2022, when the news website CoinDesk reported that Alameda held a substantial portion of its balance sheet in the FTX proprietary token, FTT. The circulating supply of this token was $5.1 billion, and Alameda held around $6 billion of the FTT token in its reserves. These reserves were the collateral against which Alameda was able to borrow money to cover its trading positions If the price of the token were to collapse, then Alameda would effectively be insolvent and unable to repay the money it had borrowed.

The leaked balance sheet information released by CoinDesk revealed a fatal weakness in Alameda's balance sheet, indicating that anyone holding the FTT token could face a substantial loss if Alameda were forced to sell its FTT tokens into the market.

As this logically played out, holders of large sums of FTT were able to run their own game theory and arrive at the conclusion that it would be in their best interests to sell their FTT before everyone else arrived at the same idea and caused its price to collapse.

As the fight between SBF and CZ intensified, it spilled over into the public domain, with SBF openly taunting CZ on Twitter over allegations that CZ would face arrest if he ever entered the US, while Bankman-Fried was already there and closing in on getting full regulatory clearance in from US regulators.

On the 6th November, CZ tweeted that in light of the Alameda balance sheet revelations, and the increasingly sour relationship between Binance and FTX, Binance would begin selling the several billion dollars' worth of FTT it had acquired from selling its investment stake in FTX in 2021.

This further added incentive to FTT holders to immediately sell their tokens, as the already perilous situation had become significantly worse due to a substantial holder indicating their intention to sell. FTX saw substantial outflows of capital and the FTT token saw significant selling pressure. Many people viewed this as a targeted and coordinated attack on FTX by CZ in order to take out a competitor. SBF took to Twitter to assure users that all was well and the company was robust. Secretly, he was frantically trying to raise money from investors to plug the increasingly large hole in FTXs balance sheet from the loans it had made to Alameda to prop up its bad trades.

Cornered and with nowhere to go, SBF went back to CZ, cap in hand, and begged for Binance to purchase FTX in its entirety. The hole in the balance sheet was too significant to cover, and the exchange was rapidly running out of money as clients withdrew funds.

Less than 2 days after the initial tweet announcing the sell off of the FTT token, CZ announced on Twitter that Binance had engaged in non-binding discussions...backstop all of the exchange's liquidity issues.

A day later, however, CZ announced again via Twitter that, having been given full access to the accounting at FTX, the hole in the balance sheet was far too substantial for Binance to purchase the company and that no rescue would be coming. The price of the FTT token had crashed by more than 80%, and the hole in FTX's balance sheet from the loans it had made to Alameda was reported to be somewhere between $8-10 billion. The withdrawals of funds from FTX were several billion dollars per day, and the exchange was rapidly approaching total insolvency. FTX suspended all withdrawals on the 9th November, as the SEC and CFTC in the US both announced they had begun formal investigations into the company.

At the time of suspension, I had around $30,000 on FTX, mostly in bitcoin and USD, and all attempts to withdraw them were unsuccessful. To date, I have the withdrawal request confirmation email sitting in my email inbox.

On the 11th November 2022, I was in Kuala Lumpur...with my partner, when I turned on the TV and saw the breaking news headline on Bloomberg.

FTX declared Chapter 11 bankruptcy.

The chain of events put in motion by the collapse of Luna had fully taken down FTX and wiped hundreds of billions of dollars off the cryptocurrency market.

For several days after the suspension of withdrawals for users, those registered as being residents of the Bahamas were still able to make withdrawals as part of an interim plea agreement that FTX made with the government of the Bahamas. The company was headquartered there, and most of the senior employees lived in the country. It has been implied that this was to allow any Bahamian users, some of whom may have been regulators and law enforcement, to withdraw their funds in full and avoid any financial loss.

This was noticed and exploited by many users by finding a Bahamas-registered user and having them withdraw balances on their behalf, for a fee. This worked as FTX had the ability to create NFTs within the platform and then sell them internally to other users. As trading was still, incredibly, not closed, a user could sell all of their assets for USD and then have the Bahamas resident create an NFT and then buy it from them for the value of the entire balance of the non-Bahamas resident's USD holdings. This effectively transferred the USD from a non-Bahamas resident to a Bahamas resident, allowing it to be withdrawn in full.

Ironically, Algod—the same individual who had made the bet highlighting issues leading to the collapse of Luna—was the most prominent user to do this, even openly asking on Twitter for a Bahamas FTX user to assist him.

SBF and the senior leaders of FTX were ultimately arrested and extradited to the US, where they all faced multiple charges. On March 28th 2024, SBF was sentenced to 25 years in federal prison for fraud; the other senior managers have all cooperated with the authorities in building the case against SBF and, at the time of writing, have yet to be sentenced.

Equally ironically, CZ was ultimately arrested by US authorities for violations of the Bank Secrecy Act and pleaded guilty. CZ was sentenced to four months' imprisonment and a $50 million fine on the 30th April 2024.

Both CZ and SBF made themselves among the richest people in the world, then publicly fought over pride and ego and over who deserved to control more of the market and have the most power and money. Both are currently sitting in federal prison cells where any amount of money and power are worth nothing.

Throughout all of the above scams, the Bitcoin blockchain continued to produce blocks and enable the transfer of value. The Bitcoin protocol was never hacked or exploited. All of the hacks and scams were the results of human failings such as greed, envy, and pride.

Bitcoin remains a neutral tool that can be used for good or ill, but far too often, many people mistake the scams and frauds carried out by people using Bitcoin as a failing of the system itself rather than a failing of the people using it.

12

Bitcoin usage in Crime

> *"The secret ingredient is crime."*
> *— Super Hans*

A common criticism of bitcoin is that it is favoured by criminals and that its only use case is in crime. Whilst I hope that the content of this book stands as a testament against that idea, it is, however, true that bitcoin is frequently used in the execution of many cybercrimes.

The very same properties that make bitcoin attractive and useful for legitimate commerce make it appealing to those who would seek to use it for nefarious intent. The pseudo-anonymity of Bitcoin wallets that provides transaction privacy for legitimate users hinders the identification of bad actors. The immutability of transactions that provides finality for purchases makes it impossible to reverse thefts. The open and permissionless nature of the Bitcoin network that allows anyone to use it means that it cannot prevent criminals from using it.

The Silk Road

One of the most prominent uses of Bitcoin in a criminal enterprise is the case of the dark-web marketplace known as 'The Silk Road'. Founded in early 2011, 'The Silk Road' was an online marketplace that specialised in the sale of illegal drugs and other illegal items such as false IDs, credit card details, and more. The marketplace operated like some combination of eBay and Amazon, in that anyone could make an account as either a buyer or a seller and list products for sale or purchase goods listed by others. The marketplace relied on a star rating system where verified buyers could review the goods and services they received from sellers, which incentivised honesty among thieves within the system; even though all parties were operating outside of the law, the financial incentives aligned so that each participant benefited more from being honest than by attempting to cheat or game the system—much like Bitcoin.

Accessing the marketplace was only possible by using the computer network known as 'The Onion Router'—also known as 'Tor'. The 'Tor' system works by connecting your device to a network of other devices running the software, and bouncing the connection between you and the external internet via a number of computers on the network. This system of connecting via multiple layers further obfuscates the origin of the request (you) and gives the system its name—each layer being like the layers of an onion.

Much like Bitcoin, the 'Tor' network is open, permissionless, anonymous, and censorship-resistant. Whilst the technical implementations differ, the end effect of providing permissionless, anonymous, censorship-free access to information has many parallels with Bitcoin. As such, the 'Tor' network is widely used by criminals, much as the Bitcoin network is also open to abuse by criminals.

The full story of 'The Silk Road' and its ultimate demise is covered in great detail in the book American Kingpin by Nick Bilton, but the key takeaways from the story are as follows:

Following months of tenacious police work from almost every three-letter US agency you can think of (FBI, DEA, IRS, DOJ, etc.), the founder and mastermind of the illegal marketplace, who went by the alias 'Dread Pirate Roberts', was eventually identified as 29-year-old Ross Ulbricht, living in San Francisco. Ulbricht was ultimately uncovered as the man behind the project due to a post he had made on an internet forum years before when he was seeking help with the idea of building a darknet marketplace, where he had used an email address connected to his real-life identity. Having placed Ulbricht under surveillance for some time and tying his real-world activity with digital logs they were able to access from the marketplace, law enforcement had sufficient evidence to tie Ulbricht to the screen name 'Dread Pirate Roberts' and moved in to arrest him. Understanding that seizing Ulbricht's laptop in an open and logged-in state would be key, given that it would be difficult, if not impossible, to break into the device were it not logged in, law enforcement conducted an operation that seems straight from a Hollywood movie. On the 1st October 2013, law enforcement followed Ulbricht to a branch of the San Francisco Public Library and waited for him to open his laptop, enter all of the required credentials, and log into 'The Silk Road'.

Unbeknownst to Ulbricht, standing nearby in the quiet library were two FBI agents who, upon receiving the nod that Ulbricht was logged in, immediately began a boisterous verbal and physical altercation. As planned, this caused Ulbricht to become distracted from his laptop, looking up at the altercation and diverting his attention. At that point, a third FBI agent swooped in and seized the laptop from the distracted Ulbricht, in its fully logged-in and open state. This was followed immediately by a further swarm of law enforcement officers to apprehend and arrest Ulbricht.

Following legal proceedings, Ulbricht was sentenced in May 2015. In what, in my opinion, stands as a damning condemnation of the barbarity of the US justice system, Ulbricht was sentenced to two life sentences plus 40 additional years without the prospect of parole. Short of any presidential intervention, Ulbricht will spend the rest of his natural-born life in a high-security prison.

Ulbricht remains a cause célèbre among many in the Bitcoin community, with many people protesting for his release, whilst others feel that his involvement in what he believed to be executions of his rivals, with hired hitmen (they were actually undercover law enforcement agents attempting to identify him), make him a flawed hero at best and a heinous criminal at worst. At its peak, 'The Silk Road' held some 614,000 bitcoin, today worth in excess of $40 billion.

In May 2024, Donald Trump publicly declared that if elected to be the 47th US President, he would commute Ulbricht's sentence 'on day one'.

Corrupt Law Enforcement

Unfortunately, a common theme in the world of Bitcoin is that the lines between good and bad are often blurred and murky. The story of Bitcoin is certainly one of flawed heroes and lovable rogues. This is no more true than in the story of the investigation and prosecution of 'The Silk Road'.

A key figure in the investigation of 'The Silk Road' was DEA agent Carl Force of the Baltimore field office in Maryland. Force worked undercover on the investigation and posed as a career criminal with connections to the crime world, using the alias 'Nob'. Force successfully ingratiated himself with Ulbricht at the illegal marketplace and built a close relationship with him during the course of the investigation. However, Force ultimately went rogue and began running operations outside the remit of his investigation, even going so far as to sell information about the investigation to Ulbricht, claiming it was from a corrupt police associate.

Aside from selling information to Ulbricht, Force would extort him for bitcoin and engage in outright theft of bitcoin from the platform. In total, Force was alleged to have stolen or otherwise dishonestly appropriated around 1,500 bitcoin, worth approximately $92 million at the time of writing.

In a similar theme, a US Secret Service agent by the name of Shaun Bridges, tasked with investigating 'The Silk Road', also went rogue during the course of his duties and embezzled as much as 20,000 bitcoin, worth some $1.2 billion at the time of writing.

Bridges seemingly believed that the US government lacked sufficient understanding of Bitcoin to detect him moving some of the bitcoin seized from 'The Silk Road' into wallets he anonymously held.

Carl Force was sentenced to some seven years in prison, whilst Shaun Bridges received a total of nine years in prison upon further sentencing for additional charges.

Evidence of the criminality of those investigating the case was not made available to the jury in deciding the case of Ross Ulbricht.

Ransomware

Whilst Bitcoin is now fairly well known in the public consciousness, that was not always so, and one of the more common ways in which people historically first heard of Bitcoin, unfortunately, was through crimes such as ransomware attacks.

Ransomware is the name given to a relatively new type of cyber-attack that really came to prominence over the last 15–20 years. In such attacks, a hacker infects a victim's system with a virus that cryptographically encrypts the contents of the device and demands a fee for decrypting those contents. Similar to the way in which bitcoin can only be moved by using the cryptographic private key of the address in which they sit, the attack maliciously and intentionally locks up the contents of the infected device with a cryptographic key known only to the attacker, who alone has the ability to decrypt those files and restore access. The name 'ransomware' comes from the idea that the attacker takes control of your system's files and agrees to release them only upon payment of a ransom.

When executed correctly, once the files are encrypted, decrypting them is as impossible as signing a Bitcoin transaction for which you do not hold the private key. In many cases where this relates to corporate machines holding vital documents, the ransom is indeed often paid; however this is perhaps akin to paying a ransom for kidnapped hostages and thus encourages further kidnapping.

Typically, the entry point for such ransomware can be through lurking the murkier parts of the internet, such as pornography or pirated content-sharing websites. More sophisticated instances of ransomware will utilise networks to spread from a single infected device to others and replicate onto machines that potentially have never even had internet access. Most commonly, the attacks prey on machines that are not updated with the latest versions of software and exploit vulnerabilities in their software to execute the attack. A timely reminder, if ever there was one, to stop snoozing on the software update notifications on your laptop.

These types of cyber-attack are not unique to Bitcoin and, in fact, pre-date Bitcoin's existence. They certainly pre-date its wider public understanding and usage. From personal experience, I remember that while living in Berlin in 2010, my laptop was struck by an attack that locked me out of the system and demanded payment to restore access. The attack demanded that I head to a petrol station and purchase redeemable gift cards equivalent to the ransom amount, and then share the redeemable codes from the cards, thereby transferring value anonymously over the internet to the attackers. Obviously, I did not comply and was able to restore my device without paying. The requirement to physically go to a point of sale and purchase redeemable gift cards presents several barriers to this attack. Most people would not physically walk to a location to buy gift cards; the in-person shame or embarrassment of purchasing a large volume of gift cards may prevent victims from doing so. Additionally, anyone purchasing a large volume or value of gift cards could be easily identified by sales staff as a potential victim, allowing them to intervene in the transaction.

This method of purchasing gift cards and transferring the codes remains popular today among, predominantly Indian based, confidence scams where a scammer calls a victim claiming to be from the tax authority or other position of authority and demanding immediate payment under penalty of arrest. The gift cards in this case are legitimate methods of value transfer being misused by criminals for nefarious purposes, but nobody suggests that the gift card industry itself is aligned with these criminals or to blame for the criminality.

Given the limitations of transferring money anonymously online using gift cards, the emergence of Bitcoin into the public consciousness made it a natural progression for ransomware attacks to begin demanding payment in bitcoin. Whilst some ransomware attacks still demand payment in gift cards and via other methods, the past decade has seen a marked shift towards Bitcoin being the primary payment method demanded in such attacks.

Today, many of the most high-profile attacks of this kind are believed to be carried out by sophisticated hacking groups, some of which are suspected to have ties to nation-states like North Korea and Russia.

Colonial Pipeline

Some examples of high-profile ransomware attacks that demanded bitcoin as payment are the Colonial Pipeline attack of May 2021 and the WannaCry attack of May 2017.

In the Colonial Pipeline attack, hackers broke into the systems of the Colonial Pipeline organisation, which was responsible for approximately 45% of all energy supplies across the East Coast of the United States. The attackers demanded 75 bitcoin in ransom, which at the time was worth approximately $4.4 million. Having weighed up the cost of the downtime on the organisation versus the ransom, the CEO made the decision to pay and obtain the key to unlock the files on their network. Whilst the hackers are typically incentivised to provide reliable decryption to victims who pay the ransom (so as to encourage other victims to pay), in this case, the decryption process was painfully slow and still caused substantial damage to the company. Interestingly, in this case, the attack was attributed to a group known as 'DarkSide'. Due to less-than-professional handling of the Bitcoin by the attackers, combined with them already being under surveillance by the FBI, 63.7 bitcoin was recovered from the attackers. The specific details of how they were able to obtain the private key to the bitcoin have not been disclosed.

WannaCry

Perhaps one of the most prominent instances of ransomware that gained broader public awareness was the 'WannaCry' attack of May 2017.

This attack exploited a vulnerability in a Microsoft messaging system that was installed by default on Windows devices. The vulnerability had been detected by the US National Security Agency (NSA), which, as is standard operating procedure for intelligence agencies, withheld disclosure of the vulnerability—known as a 'zero-day' exploit (since the software provider is unaware of the exploit and has thus had zero days to fix it)—with the intention of using it later against a hostile target.

The NSA developed software to exploit the vulnerability, creating a package known as EternalBlue. At some point in 2016, a large number of files from the NSA were leaked to a hacker group known as the Shadow Brokers, either intentionally or unintentionally. The Shadow Brokers ultimately released the EternalBlue software to the public in April 2017 as an example of the software they had obtained from the leaked NSA files. Whilst the source of the NSA data leaks to the Shadow Brokers has never been confirmed, an NSA employee named Harold T. Martin III was arrested on August 31st, 2016, for having exfiltrated 50 terabytes of data from the organisation. Many suspect this to be the source of the leak, either intentionally or recklessly.

Whilst Microsoft issued a software patch in April 2017 for the vulnerability, it was not widely adopted by the time of the attack in May 2017.

The WannaCry attack was carried out in May of 2017, and infected several million devices globally. The attack demanded $300 in bitcoin in order to receive the decryption key, which rose to $600 if not paid within three days of infection.

Among the largest victims of the attack was the National Health Service (NHS) in the UK, which suffered a substantial disruption to operations as the attack was able to propagate across many thousands of devices on its network. Whilst the attack was global and not targeted at the NHS, its effect on the British health service was substantial, leading to over 19,000 cancelled appointments and rendering key diagnostic equipment such as MRI machines inoperative. The total impact to the NHS would eventually be reported as in the region of £92 million.

The attack was eventually stopped on May 12th when British cybersecurity consultant Marcus Hutchins was able to examine the code of the attack and isolate a domain name (website address) that the malicious code referenced as an apparent 'kill switch' before it encrypted the contents of victims' devices. As part of the program, the code sent a request to iuqerfsodp9ifjap osdfjhgosurijfaewrwergwea.com, and if it received no response, it would proceed. Hutchins registered the address iuqerfsodp9i fjaposdfjhgosurijfaewrwergwea.com as part of his debugging efforts. Since the malicious code now received a response from that address, it ceased encrypting target machines and was rendered inactive.

This propelled Hutchins to global recognition, leading WIRED magazine to brand him as the 'Hacker that saved the Internet'. However, proving that no good deed goes unpunished, Hutchins was arrested by the FBI three months later whilst visiting the US for involvement with a computer virus he had worked on as an adolescent—an activity not uncommon among cybersecurity experts. Faced with up to nine years in a federal prison, Hutchins was offered a deal that would involve no jail time if he provided information on other hackers he had contact with; he declined and was ultimately sentenced to 'time served' by a judge who understood he had turned a corner and was now clearly using his abilities for the public good.

State Sanctioned Hackers

Given what we already know of human nature, combined with the state of the world as we find it today, it should come as no surprise that some rogue nations leverage Bitcoin to their own ends. Given that John McCain once described Russia as:

> 'A Gas Station Run by a Mafia That Is Masquerading as a Country'

> — John McCain

Unsurprisingly, two of the most prominent countries linked to state-sanctioned hacking involving Bitcoin are North Korea and the Russian Federation.

North Korea

By far the most prevalent and successful state sponsor of bitcoin hacking is alleged to be the Democratic People's Republic of Korea, more commonly known as 'North Korea'.

North Korea has been under some of the strongest sanctions from the international community for several decades and has significant barriers to accessing hard currency (namely US dollars [USD] or euros [EUR]) through the channels open to most other countries. Having visited North Korea for a week in 2013, I can readily attest to the idea that it is very much a 'hermit kingdom' isolated from the rest of the world; it is by some margin the most unusual country I have ever been to. Visitors are prevented from handling local currency and are required to pay for their stay and expenses in USD, which the country uses as one of its methods to obtain elusive hard foreign currencies.

In late November 2014, ostensibly in retaliation for releasing the movie 'The Interview' which lampooned the North Korean government and its leader Kim Jong Un, Sony Pictures Group suffered a substantial cyber attack that released millions of pieces of confidential data, including unreleased movies and the personal financial details of employees, among other information.

The attack was later attributed to a known hacking group known as 'Lazarus Group', who are believed to operate under the Bureau 121 arm of the North Korean intelligence agency known as the Reconnaissance General Bureau (RGB).

In the decade since the Sony Pictures hack, the Lazarus Group has been strongly linked with many high-profile attacks targeting cryptocurrency exchanges and ransomware attacks demanding payment in bitcoin. The most prominent of these is perhaps the WannaCry attack mentioned earlier in this chapter. Whilst the WannaCry attack had the widest impact on the general public, its estimated $130,000 in revenue generated makes it far from its most financially successful.

Further attacks against cryptocurrency companies include the 2018 hack of the Japanese cryptocurrency exchange Coincheck, which saw the group exploit the exchange to steal approximately $530 million of non-bitcoin cryptocurrency. The group was later linked to an even more lucrative attack in March 2022, when it is believed that they compromised the integrity of the Ronin network, a sidechain of the Ethereum network, and were able to steal approximately $620 million of Ether and other cryptocurrencies from the network.

Aside from targeting large institutions, the group is also believed to target retail investors who hold their cryptocurrency themselves, by means of browser hacks and other exploits.

In recent years, the group is even believed to have worked undercover within crypto projects by pretending to be free-lance workers in the United States and working remotely at cryptocurrency companies to build backdoors into the systems, which they later exploited to steal funds. In a sophisticated attack, North Korean agents have been known to successfully compromise US nationals to steal the identities of US individuals for Lazarus Group hackers to assume and to store laptops in their houses in the US. The group would remotely connect to these devices, thus giving detection systems the external appearance that the devices and the remote employees were located in the United States. In May 2024, an American woman by the name of Christina Chapman was arrested on suspicion of stealing 60 identities and assisting North Korean hackers in working at US cryptocurrency companies, as well as attempting to obtain US government tenders. As a result of this, some cryptocurrency companies that hire remote workers now request interviewees to publicly condemn the North Korean government and Kim Jong Un—something no North Korean would ever be able to do—as part of their candidate screening process. There are a handful of examples on social media of companies finding North Korean applicants through this method and the hilarity of them scrambling to cover any evidence of themselves when presented with the request to disparage the North Korean leadership.

Russian Federation

Whilst North Korea is significantly the largest state-backed hacking group that exploits cryptocurrency, there are also very credible reports from intelligence agencies that tie the government of the Russian Federation to some prominent cyberattacks involving cryptocurrency. In the case of the Colonial Pipeline attack mentioned earlier in this chapter, the group responsible was determined to be the hacking group known as 'DarkSide'. Further investigations from the FBI and other agencies uncovered evidence that the group was predominantly Russian-speaking and operated either directly out of Russia or one of the closely connected former Soviet Union states. Whilst there are no signs of direct involvement from the government of the Russian Federation in the attacks by groups such as 'DarkSide', it is broadly understood that such groups operate with the tacit approval and understanding of an implied non-prosecution agreement from the government, given that the groups target the interests of Russia's geopolitical rivals.

Terrorist Financing

Given the permissionless and censorship-resistant nature of the Bitcoin network, the ability for any party to transfer value to any other party pseudo-anonymously gives the entire system its value, but also means that it is effectively impossible to prevent the same system from being used by bad actors such as terrorist financiers.

The most prominent examples of this include the proscribed terrorist groups 'Hamas' and 'Palestinian Islamic Jihad', operating primarily out of the Gaza Strip and West Bank regions of the Palestinian Territories. Beginning in 2019, the group Hamas, via its military wing 'Izz ad-Din al-Qassam', began to solicit donations in bitcoin through its social media channels.

The group touted the donations as being 'anonymous' and untraceable, whilst also taking steps to avoid detection by continuously using freshly generated Bitcoin wallet addresses that are not connected to previous addresses. However, whilst the Bitcoin network itself does not require any identification of senders or recipients, the access points by which one can buy or sell bitcoin now almost universally require strict 'Know Your Customer' (KYC) processes that identify and verify the details of the buyer or seller. Given the public and open nature of the Bitcoin blockchain, this makes the tracing of funds public and easy to accomplish.

The US and Israeli intelligence began tracking and tracing funds associated with the Bitcoin wallet addresses of the terrorist groups. By working with blockchain analytics firms such as Chainalysis, Elliptic, and CipherTrace, they were able to follow the flows of bitcoin back to their point of purchase by the donor and through to the point of sale for fiat currency on the recipient's side. By working with the cryptocurrency exchanges on both ends of the process, the intelligence agencies were able to both identify individuals connected with the illicit funding and freeze and ultimately seize the vast majority of the bitcoin involved in the entire donation process.

Due to enhanced enforcement and the identification of donors involved, both groups stopped soliciting donations using cryptocurrency in 2021, and have not resumed in any meaningful way since. The pseudo-anonymous nature of the Bitcoin blockchain, combined with the public broadcasting of all transactions and the KYC requirements on exchanges, essentially rendered the use of bitcoin for terrorist financing too difficult to execute and the risk of large-scale seizures too high to be viable at any meaningful scale for terrorist organisations.

Coin Mixers

One of the primary methods used in laundering funds in Bitcoin is the use of coin mixers, also sometimes referred to as 'tumblers', to break the traceability of bitcoins and obfuscate the transaction history of individual bitcoins.

As covered previously, all transactions on the Bitcoin blockchain are public and inherently traceable by nature. Nothing can be done from a technical point of view to change that, aside from potentially using some side-chain or Layer 2 solutions to transfer bitcoin. However, coin mixers exist as a service to break the traceability of individual bitcoins by pooling them with volumes of other, mostly legitimate, bitcoin in a single holding wallet and then distributing them to new wallet addresses that are held by the original bitcoin holders.

Perhaps the best way to explain the functioning of a coin mixer is by means of an example:

Imagine you have 100 bitcoin you wish to hide the provenance of; this could be funds stolen from a hack, or simply money you received from someone that you wish to prevent them from knowing how and where you spend it.

You could take the 100 bitcoin and send them to a coin mixer, whilst also providing a list of freshly generated Bitcoin wallet addresses that are unconnected to the wallet you made the deposit from. The coin mixer then takes in thousands of bitcoins in deposits from hundreds or thousands of entirely unconnected users, some with criminal origin, but many with legitimate privacy intentions, and holds them all in one wallet.

The mixer may charge a fee of 1–3%, so in this example, we will assume a 1% fee for the sake of simplicity. The mixer then holds onto all of your bitcoin and the bitcoin from the multiple other users, whilst noting your deposit amount and the list of new addresses to which you wish to receive your paid out bitcoin.

In this case, the mixer may make payment in individual transactions over several hours or days in randomised amounts from the main wallet in which all of the deposited bitcoin is held.

In this example, assuming we deposited 100 bitcoin and provided ten fresh wallet addresses to receive the laundered funds, the mixer may pay out something similar to the following:
Hour 1: New Bitcoin address 4: 24 bitcoin
Hour 4: New Bitcoin address 8: 10 bitcoin
Hour 5: New Bitcoin address 2: 4 bitcoin
Hour 7: New Bitcoin address 10: 30 bitcoin
Hour 9: New Bitcoin address 3: 5 bitcoin
Hour 12: New Bitcoin address 5: 26 bitcoin

The net result is the receipt of 99 bitcoin (100 bitcoin minus a 1% fee) to six freshly generated and unconnected wallets, of which you hold the private keys to spend the received bitcoin.

Whilst the on-chain traceability of bitcoin remains intact, the record will show bitcoin being deposited into the mixer by someone (possibly your own deposited bitcoin, but more likely bitcoin deposited by another user) and then being paid out to a brand new wallet.

By splitting the amount paid out into randomised sub-amounts of the total and paying it to multiple unconnected wallets, it would be impossible for anyone to track on the chain that you received a total of 99 bitcoin, as the payouts are all for amounts smaller than 99 bitcoin and are also made to multiple unconnected wallets. At the same time, other users are also receiving payouts to wallets in various amounts.

Coin mixers like this are able to operate only if they are used by non-criminals who seek simply to break the trace of their bitcoin in order to afford themselves more privacy in their affairs. This is a valid use case and has historically been useful for Bitcoin users to achieve greater privacy. However, the illicit use of coin mixers makes them a target for law enforcement, and many exchanges have begun to adopt policies of seizing any bitcoins that have interacted with coin mixers and, at a minimum, conducting deeper KYC checks and questions as to the provenance of the bitcoin deposited to the exchange before releasing them. This ultimately entirely undoes the work of the anonymising mixing service in the first place.

Coin mixers come in two different types: centralised and de-centralised. Centralised mixers require a trusted third party to take custody of the coins and then issue the payments, which increases risk as the third party may run away with the bitcoin or otherwise not make payments. Given that a primary use of mixers is concealing funds and preserving anonymity, many users would be unlikely to complain to authorities in the event of having their bitcoin stolen, which makes using centralised mixers a very high-risk activity.

Decentralised mixers are therefore preferable and typically work using an open-source algorithm to handle deposits and payments in a way that maintains the privacy of the whole system. Typically, this is achieved using a consensus-based algorithm and multiple unconnected nodes working together to verify and process deposits and payouts. The open-source nature of these systems and the lack of a single centralised entity significantly reduce the risk of losing funds to a malicious actor during the process.

Personally, I have never had cause to use a bitcoin mixer, and with the increased surveillance of them and the increased frequency of most major exchanges and protocols to seize any bitcoin connected to a mixer, they have become less and less viable for most lawful users of Bitcoin.

For the most part, simply breaking the string of on-chain surveillance of your bitcoin can be done by depositing it to an exchange and then withdrawing it to a new address. In this case, the exchange itself does have a record of your bitcoin movement, but the public network does not. For most legal purposes, this should be enough to provide an acceptable level of privacy, isolating the knowledge of the flow of funds to a single exchange which would not ordinarily be compelled to disclose it without a qualified legal demand from law enforcement.

Simply acquiring bitcoin without any KYC trace is still possible by purchasing bitcoin in person via face-to-face meetings for cash, though those are not without their risks such as robbery or fraud. Realistically, these methods are only viable for small amounts of money, certainly below $500,000 at a time in my experience.

Whilst bitcoin mixers have been a staple feature of the Bitcoin world and used by countless thousands of people, as the industry matures and surveillance increases, the viability of such tools continues to decrease.

As with many aspects of privacy, concealing the origin of your bitcoin is a spectrum of the effort you are willing to go to and the level of privacy you seek to achieve. For most users, simply using a centralised entity such as an exchange should be broadly sufficient, but more complex ideas could include using coin mixers, bridging your bitcoin to wrapped bitcoin on other chains such as Ethereum, selling the bitcoin for Ethereum, using Ethereum coin mixers, selling the Ether for wrapped bitcoin, bridging it back to a fresh wallet, etc. The level of viability of these methods also decreases with the volume of the bitcoin you are seeking to anonymise.

Whilst the Bitcoin network is undoubtedly used in criminality, it remains a very small fraction of the overall use, with the volume of total cryptocurrency transactions connected with criminality in 2023 being estimated at a mere 0.34% of total volume, according to a report by Chainalysis. The open and public nature of transactions provides some barrier to its use for illicit purposes, as seen by the examples of terrorist financing.

By any measure, the vast majority of financial crimes continue to use traditional finance networks and predominantly the US dollar as their primary methods of exchange.

13

The Future of Bitcoin

> "The future is already here – it's just not very evenly distributed."
> — William Gibson

In the mere fifteen years since its inception, Bitcoin has already achieved some significant milestones and shot into global consciousness as something of a household name. We have gone from an obscure internet quirk hacked together by nerds in their basement, to the leading candidate of the 2024 presidential election delivering a keynote speech at the world's most prominent Bitcoin conference, promising to stockpile bitcoin as a strategic reserve of the United States government.

We now have BlackRock running a bitcoin ETF that quickly became the fastest-growing ETF in history by a country mile and multi-billion-dollar public companies holding bitcoin as a reserve asset on their balance sheets. We have nation-states adopting bitcoin as national legal tender and going toe-to-toe with the IMF over their insistence on holding bitcoin as a national reserve and currency.

Whilst for many in the Bitcoin community, the day-to-day progress often feels slow and underwhelming, the progress we can see looking back over the last five, ten, or fifteen years is more than anyone could have realistically dreamed of at the start of those periods. Such is human nature, as succinctly described by Bill Gates.

> "Most people overestimate what they can do in one year and underestimate what they can do in ten years."
> — Bill Gates

Most people talk about the future of Bitcoin only in predictions of its future price. From terminally online crypto bros on X to multinational banks writing opinion pieces or newsletters. Personally, I don't tend to be drawn into making price predictions; the odds of being wrong significantly outweigh the odds of being correct, and if asked, I typically reply with the line 'bitcoin price predictions are like nipples, everyone's got one'.

What we can do, however, is look at the broader ecosystem and political landscape, and get some indication of where the industry might be headed in the next fifteen years, even with the understanding that those predictions are likely to end up being wide of the mark.

De-Dollarisation

A pervasive theme in international finance for the past decade or so has been the idea of global 'de-dollarisation' whereby the world will transition away from the use of the US dollar as the main global currency. As we covered in the opening chapter of this book, the US dollar has been the global reserve asset and primary global unit of exchange since the end of the Cold War, and the Bretton Woods agreement. Global trade in hydrocarbons such as crude oil, natural gas, and more has been almost entirely denominated in US dollars for the majority of the last century, even giving rise to the term 'petrodollar' among some critics. This reliance on the dollar as the global unit of account has caused frustration, not least among some of the United States geopolitical adversaries as they are forced to purchase US dollars in order to buy the oil and gas that forms the lifeblood of modern economies. Even today, China purchases oil in US dollars, and the Russian Federation, much as it presumably loathes to, is forced to sell its oil in US dollars. In fact, the sweeping sanctions on Russia in the wake of the war in Ukraine included specific carveouts in the texts to permit certain Russian banks to process US dollars lest the entire global energy trade grind to a halt overnight.

Whilst countries may bemoan the use of the dollar and wish for an alternative, the fact is that the US dollar remains in an overwhelmingly dominant position and is hard to dislodge from its current standing due to the level at which it is already entrenched in the global financial systems. Moreover, there is still no viable alternative that could replace it at the moment. Russia could sell its oil priced in rubles, but any nation purchasing it would rightfully demand a deep discount to make the trade worthwhile, given they would need to acquire rubles first. Additionally, any such trade would be small and limited, as no country would feel comfortable holding a large amount of rubles on its balance sheet. Following the sanctions bonanza on Russia in 2022, the Russian government saw fit to tear up billions of dollars' worth of international agreements and seize businesses and property within the country, which certainly does nothing to endear third parties to hold its currency.

China could use its purchasing might to demand that global contracts be denominated in the Chinese yuan, but the currency remains fairly closed and protected. Additionally, there are significant difficulties in acquiring the yuan in large volumes outside of China, with capital controls strictly limiting any flow of yuan outside the country.

The US itself is certainly not without fault and is seen by many as having weaponised its position as the governor of the global currency, from its draconian dragnet legislation such as FATCA (which requires all banks globally to report its customers to the US government) to its seizure of $300 billion of Russian government assets and its removal of Russia from the global SWIFT banking network. There are no heroes in this story. There are increasing reasons for countries to want to remove themselves from the US dollar system, but at the same time the geopolitical alternatives also continue to make themselves less appealing.

Many in the Bitcoin world suggest that Bitcoin itself is the only viable alternative as a global reserve currency. Whilst that may be true at some point in the future, as of today that remains unworkable and unfeasible with the current level of maturity and development of the network.

BRICS

An idea that gained some traction in the past few years was that a group of countries might come together to issue their own collective currency to rival the global usage of the US dollar. These countries were often referred to using the acronym 'BRICS' after their constituent countries:

Brazil
Russia
India
China
South Africa

A somewhat bizarre, rag-tag group of countries that seem to share little in common other than a desire to move away from the US dollar. Among these countries, India and China are political adversaries that have been in conflict several times in the last century, Russia and China have a long history of violating international law, Brazil has one of the most closed domestic financial markets in the world, and South Africa is South Africa. Before any such BRICS currency could gain external recognition and acceptance, the countries would need to establish a trusted framework among themselves—something for which I would caution you not to hold your breath.

The lack of trust between internal parties is, by its very nature, inhibitive to any system in which the members require trust. Such a system is the antithesis of Bitcoin and its inherent design, which treats all other members of the network as potentially hostile by default. By removing the requirement for trust, the currency would no longer be controlled or operated by anyone, including the constituent countries of BRICS.

I cannot see an alternative BRICS currency ever materialising for a multitude of reasons, but you can test your own receptiveness to the idea of a BRICS currency by running the following thought exercise: Imagine someone owed you the equivalent of ten years' salary and offered to pay you in either:

US dollars
Brazilian Real
Russian Ruble
Indian Rupee
Chinese Yuan
South African Rand

Which would you choose? And why is it the US dollar?

CBDCs

In an interesting turn of events, having spent the previous fifteen years fighting against the emergence of blockchain technology and Bitcoin, some Western governments have recently begun to hint at the prospect of rolling out national government-controlled cryptocurrency networks. Central Bank Digital Currencies (CBDCs) have gained attention in Western countries as a polarising issue, part of a global push to move away from cash payments in pursuit of reducing illegal transactions or reducing tax evasion. In the US, CBDCs have become a partisan issue, with Democrats pushing for their introduction and Republicans standing in opposition on grounds of government surveillance and personal liberty.

Whilst the convenience of digital currency has many benefits, as with many things, there is a trade-off with the negatives that increased surveillance and censorship could usher in.

Whilst there are many downsides to cash as a means of payment—such as loss, damage, and counterfeiting—its ability to facilitate payments anonymously is perhaps unrivalled by any other widely used method today. Though this is often associated with criminality, there are also many lawful reasons that one might seek to achieve anonymity in purchases. These might range from the mundane act of purchasing a gift for a partner with whom you share a bank account, to purchasing a book that is critical of your government or donating to an opposition political movement. Whilst the latter examples might not seem very relatable to people living in a free and fair Western democratic country, for now, it could well be an important consideration for many people in less progressive regimes.

Whilst several countries have made encouraging noises towards implementing their own CBDC, most notably China, there have been only a handful of such projects rolled out globally.

Sand Dollar

The Central Bank of the Bahamas introduced the first-ever CBDC in October 2020 with the roll-out of the 'Sand Dollar,' a digital currency tied 1:1 with the Bahamian dollar. The currency is open to all Bahamas residents aged 18 or over and is legal tender within the country, for purchases both online and in person. The Sand Dollar runs on a private blockchain, which has permissioned access and is entirely owned and operated by the Bahamian Central Bank.

The permissioned and closed nature of the blockchain it operates on makes the Sand Dollar non-transferable outside of its closed ecosystem.

eNaira

A year later, in October 2021, the Nigerian Central Bank introduced their own CBDC, the 'eNaira,' pegged 1:1 with the national currency of Nigeria. Similar to the Sand Dollar, the eNaira operates on a closed and permissioned blockchain, fully owned and administered by the Central Bank of Nigeria.

In both cases, though more so in Nigeria, the CBDCs were rolled out as a reactionary measure to the popularity of Bitcoin and other cryptocurrencies in the countries where they were introduced. Nigeria has long been one of the largest bitcoin hubs in Africa, with its population showing a distrust of government, coupled with increasing technical savviness and an economy reliant on overseas remittances. A 2020 survey from

Statista showed that 32% of Nigerians reported owning or using cryptocurrency.

In an attempt to regain control of this, the Nigerian Central Bank announced a ban on all banks within the country facilitating any cryptocurrency activities. This simply pushed a majority of bitcoin trading from centralised exchanges to simple peer-to-peer transactions between individuals.

The eNaira was introduced by the Nigerian government in order to replicate many of the features of bitcoin, such as fast transactions, financial inclusion for the unbanked, seamless overseas transfers, and more, but with strong top-down government control and supervision of the entire system.

As of late 2024, the eNaira continues to struggle to gain adoption among the wider population of Nigeria, with most Nigerians preferring to use the non-government-controlled Bitcoin network.

Looking Forwards

It's hard to imagine how the next fifteen years of Bitcoin could be as impactful and disruptive as the previous fifteen years have been. The level of adoption achieved so far, is remarkable and breathtaking, but every day more people join the Bitcoin ecosystem and bring with them their own smarts, wisdom, and perspectives. Some of the smartest people I have ever met work in Bitcoin (though I'm sure there's a large dose of selection bias there).

As Satoshi himself said, the vast majority of the Bitcoin codebase was set in stone forever at the point of initial release in 2009. Any new technological development in the ecosystem today comes broadly from tinkering around the edges of the code and developing upon some of the non-core sections of the protocol. Or more commonly by developing external software that interacts with and incorporates Bitcoin into other systems.

Whilst Bitcoin is an incredible leap of technological progress and probably the single biggest innovation in finance since the introduction of banks in the 1400s, it would be foolish to consider Bitcoin in its current state to be without problems or areas that need improvement.

The current maximum capacity of transactions to achieve finality on the Bitcoin blockchain is far too low for bitcoin to be used widely by seven billion people around the world. This can be, and broadly is, solved to some degree by Layer 2 solutions such as the Lightning Network and other technologies covered in previous chapters of this book. The general usability of Bitcoin, for most people remains somewhat awkward and daunting, with addresses given as long strings of non-human-readable text that are technically sound but jarring to many potential users. The issues around personal custody are troublesome for many non-technical users. One private key is susceptible to theft or attack, and multi-key solutions are technologically daunting. In general, the level of fraud and theft in the space is far too high for most people to contend with.

Whilst some of these problems have technical solutions, most of them are human interface issues. We talk in the Bitcoin space of Layer 1 being the Bitcoin blockchain and Layer 2 being side-chains or sub-chains that exist below the main blockchain, and we take some pride in the idea that Bitcoin is the single most dominant of all Layer 1 solutions in the cryptocurrency space, which has certainly been part of the main battle for the past decade or more.

The main battle for Bitcoin in the next decade won't be fought at the Layer 1 level or even the Layer 2 level; it will be fought at the Layer 0 level, the human level.

Whilst it would be foolish to rest on the technical laurels that Bitcoin has achieved so far, constant improvement and diligence are absolutely required going forward to protect the protocol. It is also fair to say that the technology behind the protocol has been sufficiently battle-tested now, and the 'Lindy effect' of its longevity is cemented in the public consciousness. I think we find ourselves at something of an inflection point for Bitcoin between the early adopters, technical tinkers, nerds, and broader global public adoption.

This would be something akin to where the internet found itself some 30 years ago. In 1994, you'd have to have some understanding of TCP/IP protocols, DNS routing, and purchase dedicated hardware you'd configure yourself in order to get a poor connection to share Dungeons & Dragons stories with someone you knew 200 miles away.

The internet was indeed dismissed by critics at the time. Famously, the Nobel Prize-winning economist Paul Krugman said of the internet in 1998:

> "By 2005, it will become clear that the Internet's impact on the economy has been no greater than the fax machine's."
> – Paul Krugman

This was obviously incorrect, but had the internet remained in its 1998 state, it might have been a less outrageous prediction.

Today, you can walk into any cafe or bar in the world and the majority of them will have the internet provided to you free of charge via Wi-Fi, beamed directly to the smartphone in your pocket that is more powerful than any consumer computer available in 1998.

The internet solved the two key issues that Bitcoin faces today: scalability and usability.

I can sit in a bar in Indonesia and effortlessly scroll through photographs my grandma posted seconds ago from her holiday on the other side of the earth, and I can assure you she has never heard of TCP/IP nor would she have any need to. Technologies built on top of the internet abstracted away the technical knowledge from the usability layer, whilst the internet protocol layer continued to expand its capacity and throughput to bring on billions of users across the globe.

Bitcoin needs to continue to trend towards this direction with full force in order to reach the level of global adoption that it is ultimately capable of and arguably destined to fulfil. There are many positive moves in this direction, from increased adoption of the Lightning Network to modern local bank-style solutions built on top of the Bitcoin network, such as the great work Fedi is building with their bitcoin-powered e-money solutions.

Bitcoin has fought incredibly over the past fifteen years to go from a standing start to becoming a multi-trillion-dollar asset second only to gold in total market value. The fight has been on all levels, all the time, from getting the technical aspects correct, to achieving user adoption, to scaling, and all with strong headwinds from often corrupt and biased entrenched governments and institutions. The troubles we face as a community are far from over, and there is still much to do, but it does feel like a lot of the harder work is behind us now, in the words of Winston Churchill.

> "Now this is not the end. It is not even the beginning of the end. But it is, perhaps, the end of the beginning."
> – Winston Churchill

Bitcoin is here for the long haul. Those of us who have been in the trenches for a while have the scars to prove it. Many of us see Bitcoin adoption as an inevitability and the question is merely 'how quickly' rather than 'if'.

If the past decade is anything to go by, the path will likely be long, frustrating, troublesome, and involve fighting the same battles many times before they are won, but at this point I'm pretty sure most Bitcoiners wouldn't have it any other way.

As for what the future of Bitcoin looks like?

That's up to you.

> "I don't know the future. I didn't come here to tell you how this is going to end. I came here to tell you how it's going to begin".
> — Neo, *The Matrix*

www.ingramcontent.com/pod-product-compliance
Ingram Content Group UK Ltd.
Pitfield, Milton Keynes, MK11 3LW, UK
UKHW041953190726
13854UKWH00005B/1953